easy eats!

hamlyn

easy eats!

First published in the U.K. in 1999
by Hamlyn, a division of
Octopus Publishing Group Ltd
2–4 Heron Quays
London E14 4JP

Copyright © 1999, 2001 Octopus Publishing Group Ltd

ISBN 0 600 60467 5

Printed in Great Britain

NOTES

Both metric and imperial measurements have been given in all recipes. Use one set of measurements only and not a mixture of both.

Standard level spoon measurements are used in all recipes.
1 tablespoon = one 15 ml spoon
1 teaspoon = one 5 ml spoon

Eggs should be medium to large unless otherwise stated. The Department of Health advises that eggs should not be consumed raw. This book contains dishes made with raw or lightly cooked eggs. It is prudent for more vulnerable people such as pregnant and nursing mothers, invalids, the elderly, babies and young children to avoid uncooked or lightly cooked dishes made with eggs. Once prepared, these dishes should be kept refrigerated and used promptly.

Milk should be full fat unless otherwise stated.

Poultry should be cooked thoroughly. To test if poultry is cooked, pierce the flesh through the thickest part with a skewer or fork – the juices should run clear, never pink or red.

Do not re-freeze a dish that has been frozen previously.

Pepper should be freshly ground black pepper unless otherwise stated.

Fresh herbs should be used, unless otherwise stated. If unavailable, use dried herbs as an alternative but halve the quantities stated.

Measurements for canned food have been given as a standard metric equivalent.

Nuts and nut derivatives
This book includes dishes made with nuts and nut derivatives. It is advisable for customers with known allergic reactions to nuts and nut derivatives and those who may be potentially vulnerable to these allergies, such as pregnant and nursing mothers, invalids, the elderly, babies and children, to avoid dishes made with nuts and nut oils. It is also prudent to check the labels of pre-prepared ingredients for the possible inclusion of nut derivatives.

Ovens should be preheated to the specified temperature – if using a fan-assisted oven, follow the manufacturer's instructions for adjusting the time and the temperature.

Contents

Introduction

Easy eating is all about preparing and enjoying good food in a relaxed way with the minimum of fuss and effort. Each dish makes an ideal meal-in-one to savour when curled up in front of the television or with a good book — the ultimate in comfort food.

Cooked in a single pot or served in one bowl or on a single plate, these complete meals involve little of your attention during the cooking process and the least amount of washing up and clearing away afterwards. This all means that nothing gets in the way of your appreciation of the wide variety of delicious dishes on offer.

The concept behind this no-fuss cooking and dining has provided many of the world's cuisines with their most inimitable dishes – think of Spain's paella, Hungary's goulash, north-east America's fish chowder – and with good reason. Each brings together a unique combination of ingredients with their complementary flavours and textures, creating a rich and memorable taste experience.

In this book, you will find a wide-ranging collection of recipes for easy food of all kinds, from the soups and long-cooked casseroles that everyone warmly welcomes in the wintertime, to the quickly-made, crisp and colourful stir-fry meals of oriental origin that have universal appeal. Pasta and rice dishes feature prominently, along with hearty stews and imaginative main course salads and vegetable-based dishes. And, of course, there are recipes for updated versions of the classic dishes mentioned above, as well as a number of contemporary-style recipes that draw on the wealth of delicious and exotic ingredients that come into our shops and supermarkets from all over the world.

UTENSILS

As we have seen, many of the recipes in this book are cooked in just one pot, with the different ingredients being added at various stages of the cooking time. This allows the variety of flavours to combine and fully develop in the cooking vessel, in preparation for serving all in one bowl. There are many specialised pots and pans traditionally used for cooking these dishes, but cooks can get away with a few basic pots and pans for recipes in this book.

CASSEROLE

The casserole is probably the most basic dish used and is extremely versatile with regards to the types of dishes that can be cooked in it. The dictionary defines a casserole as a covered dish in which food is both cooked and served. It is a definition which leaves a lot to the imagination, such as; what shape, what size, what can it be made of? In fact, casseroles come in many shapes and sizes and with many functions.

The best casseroles are quite heavy and have tight-fitting lids which help keep moisture in — important when the dish is being cooked slowly for a long time. They have a handle on either side, to make lifting them easier than would be possible with one long handle (difficult for fitting into ovens, anyway). Casseroles are usually straight-sided and squat, rather than tall, a shape which means they can easily hold larger cuts and joints of meat and whole poultry and game birds and still have room for other ingredients such as vegetables, herbs, wines and stocks.

Casseroles are made from earthenware, stoneware, porcelain, stainless steel, cast iron and enamelled cast iron. There are also special oven glass and lined copper casseroles.

Many recipes in this book call for either a 'flameproof' or an 'ovenproof' casserole. There is an important difference between the two. An ovenproof casserole can only be used in an oven, whereas a flameproof one can be sat on direct heat as well as being used in the oven - very useful when some of the ingredients in a dish need preliminary browning before being put in the oven. Porcelain, stoneware, most glass and many of the earthenware casseroles are ovenproof only, though some specially fired earthenware pots can be used on direct heat, ideally in conjunction with a diffuser mat. Cast iron, enamelled cast iron and stainless steel are generally all flameproof.

A final thought about casseroles. Since they are used for both cooking and serving food, it is a good idea to choose one that looks attractive sitting on the table — which is why those lovely brown earthenware pots which are used throughout Europe or the stoneware ones of Oriental cooking are so popular.

WOK

A pan used for many recipes in this book – notably the stir-fry dishes – is the wok, for which the Western-style deep-sided frying pan makes an excellent substitute. Woks come with one long handle or two small handles: choose whichever you feel will be best for you, but make sure the wok has a close-fitting lid, to make it a more versatile pan. Frying pans, too, should have good-fitting lids.

SAUCEPAN

If your basic stove-top pot is a saucepan, make sure you have one with a good heavy base: it will sit safely on the hob and foods are less

likely to stick to the bottom than they would with a thin pan. If a really low heat cannot be obtained from your hob, use a heat diffuser mat under a saucepan being used for very slow and long cooking.

STEAMER

The steamer, or multi-pot pan, is an extremely versatile pan for stove-top one-pot cooking. Choose one with a well-fitting lid, so that steam cannot escape during cooking, and make sure that the perforated liner pan fits snugly into the bottom pan, which, ideally, should be heavy-based. The perforated pan can be used to steam vegetables, pasta, oriental dumplings and English steamed puddings above the main dish. Lined with muslin, it can also be used to steam couscous.

INGREDIENTS

Because ingredients such as vegetables and herbs play such a big part in many of the recipes in this book, it is particularly important that they are always of good quality. Newly-picked green vegetables, in particular, have much more flavour and a far better texture than vegetables that have sat around for several days after picking. Good storage conditions can help to keep ingredients fresh — a cool, dry, dark place for root vegetables is ideal, and the cool box at the bottom of the refrigerator for other vegetables, for instance.

On the whole, there is no perfect substitute for fresh, fragrant herbs,

whose glorious flavours are very much reduced and can even be changed completely when they are dried or frozen. Fortunately, supermarkets these days sell fresh herbs, either growing in pots or freshly picked and in sealed packs, all year round, so they are readily obtainable. Store cut herbs in plastic bags in the refrigerator cool box, washing them only as you are

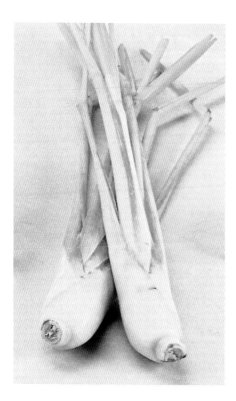

ready to use them and growing herbs can be picked and used as and when you need them.

Although spices, used to delicious effect in many recipes here, last much longer than fresh herbs, do keep an eye on the 'best before' dates on jars and packets. Spices will lose their pungency and flavour over time, and should be replaced regularly.

Two vegetables that are often used in recipes in this book to give colour, texture and particularly flavour, are tomatoes and sweet peppers, especially red peppers. Both are, more often than not, used skinned or peeled (and deseeded).

Skinning tomatoes is simple. Cut a shallow cross at the stem end of the tomato and then put it in a bowl of boiling water to cover. Leave it for about 1–2 minutes, take it out of the bowl with a slotted spoon and peel off the skin.

Carefully peel raw peppers with a vegetable peeler to take off just the thin layer of peel and none of the flesh. Alternatively, blacken peppers under a hot grill for a deliciously roasted flavour. Cut the pepper in half, remove the core and seeds and then flatten each pepper half with your hand. Put the peppers, skin side up, under a preheated, hot grill and leave until the skin is blackened and blistered. Transfer the hot pepper pieces to a plastic bag and leave them to steam in it for 2 or 3 minutes. When they are cool enough to handle, strip away the blackened skin. Alternatively, the pepper pieces can be rinsed under cold running water to remove the skin.

ADAPTING RECIPE QUANTITIES

Although most of the recipes in this book have been prepared to serve 4 or 6, quantities can be increased to serve many more. The great thing about easy eating is that as many of the recipes can be prepared in one pot or pan, it is relatively easy to adjust the ingredients to allow for extra servings. However, there are a few essential points to remember when adapting recipes:

• A simple doubling of the quantities of the ingredients in a recipe serving 4 people will provide servings for 8–10 people.

• When cooking a meat, poultry or fish dish for a number of people, where the original recipe allows 250 g (8 oz) of the basic ingredient per person, this can be reduced to 150 g (5 oz).

• Don't prepare recipes in quantities of more than times-four the original, since it is very difficult to get the balance of the flavourings right.

• When multiplying dishes which have significant amounts of herbs and spices, take special care with quantities. Never increase the amount of hot spices, in direct proportion to the original recipe: add a little, taste the result, and add more, as necessary.

HOMEMADE STOCKS

Many of the recipes in this book call for significant quantities of stock. While acceptable fresh and frozen stocks are widely available today, nothing beats the flavour of a good homemade stock. They are easily and cheaply made and, once cooked and cooled, freeze beautifully. The chicken, beef and vegetable stocks here can all be frozen for up to three months. It is a good idea to freeze stocks in small amounts, both for ease of storage and convenience in use. Freeze them in ice cube trays, then transfer the cubes to labelled and dated plastic bags.

CHICKEN STOCK

1 chicken carcass, raw or cooked
1 onion, roughly chopped
2 large carrots
1 celery stalk
1 bay leaf
a few parsley stalks
1 thyme sprig
1.8 litres (3 pints) cold water

1 Chop the chicken carcass into 3 or 4 pieces and put in a large, heavy-based saucepan with any trimmings. Add the onion, carrots, celery and bay leaf. Crush the parsley stalks lightly and add them, with the thyme. Pour over the water to cover.
2 Bring the stock to the boil, skimming off any scum that rises to the surface. Cover the pan and simmer for 2–2½ hours.
3 Strain the stock through a muslin-lined sieve and leave to cool before putting in the refrigerator. If the stock is to be frozen, cool it quickly (sit the bowl or stock in cold water, for instance) first.

Preparation time: 5–10 minutes
Cooking time: about 2½ hours
Makes 1 litre (1¾ pints)

BEEF STOCK

750 g (1½ lb) boned shin of beef, cubed
2 onions, roughly chopped
2 large carrots
2 celery sticks
1 bouquet garni (2 parsley sprigs, 2 thyme sprigs, 2 bay leaves)
4–6 black peppercorns
1.8 litres (3 pints) cold water

1 Put the cubes of beef in a large, heavy-based saucepan. Add the onions, carrots, celery, bouquet garni and peppercorns. Pour over the water.
2 Bring the stock slowly to the boil, then reduce the heat to a slow simmer. Cover the pan tightly and simmer for 4 hours, skimming off any scum from time to time.
3 Strain the stock through a muslin-lined sieve and leave to cool before storing in the refrigerator. If the stock is to be frozen, cool it quickly first.

Preparation time: 15 minutes
Cooking time: about 4½ hours
Makes about 1.5 litres (2½ pints)

VEGETABLE STOCK

For this stock, use vegetables you have available, and according to taste. Avoid using potatoes or other floury vegetables, as they will make the stock cloudy.

500 g (1 lb) mixed vegetables, chopped
1 garlic clove
1 bouquet garni (2 parsley sprigs, 2 thyme sprigs, 2 bay leaves)
1.2 litres (2 pints) cold water

1 Put the vegetables, garlic and bouquet garni in a large, heavy-based saucepan. Pour over the water.
2 Bring the stock to the boil, cover the saucepan and simmer gently for 30 minutes, skimming off any scum, if necessary.
3 Strain the stock, and cook before storing in the refrigerator, until it is needed.

Preparation time: 5–10 minutes
Cooking time: about 45 minutes
Makes 1 litre (1¾ pints)

Soups

Soups can be light and
extremely simple or they can be
a substantial meal, containing
chunky vegetables, fish and meat.
The soups in this chapter cover all
occasions, from snacks and
appetizers to main meal dishes.

Spanish Chickpea Soup

150 g (5 oz) dried chickpeas,
   soaked overnight
1 small smoked, boneless
   bacon hock joint, about
   500–750 g (1–1½ lb)
1 onion, studded with 4 cloves
2 garlic cloves, crushed
1 bay leaf
1 thyme sprig
1 marjoram sprig

1 parsley sprig
1.8 litres (3 pints) water
1.8 litres (3 pints) Chicken
   Stock (see page 9)
300–375 g (10–12 oz) potatoes,
   peeled and cut into 1 cm
   (½ inch) cubes
300 g (10 oz) Savoy cabbage,
   shredded
salt and pepper

1 Drain the chickpeas in a colander, rinse under cold running water and drain again. Put the bacon joint in a deep saucepan and cover with cold water. Bring the water briefly to the boil, then drain, discarding the water.

2 Return the bacon joint to the clean saucepan. Add the chickpeas, onion, garlic, bay leaf, thyme, marjoram, parsley and water. Bring the mixture to the boil then lower the heat and simmer, partially covered, for *1½ hours*. Remove and discard the onion, bay leaf and sprigs of thyme, marjoram and parsley. Lift out the bacon joint, place it on a board and cut it into small pieces. Set aside.

3 Add the stock, potatoes and cabbage to the pan and simmer for a further *30 minutes*. Add the reserved hock pieces to the soup and cook for *10 minutes* more. Season with salt and pepper, to taste. Serve in soup bowls.

Preparation time: 15 minutes, plus soaking
Cooking time: 2–2½ hours
Serves 8–10

Bacon and Split Pea Soup

125 g (4 oz) split peas
1 small turnip
1 carrot
2 leeks
2 tablespoons oil
8 rindless smoked streaky
   bacon rashers, diced

1.5 litres (2½ pints) ham or
   Chicken Stock (see page 9)
salt and pepper
½ teaspoon dried mixed herbs
150 ml (¼ pint) single cream
1 tablespoon chopped
   parsley, to garnish

1 Cover the split peas with cold water and soak overnight. Drain well. Dice the turnip and carrot. Slice the leeks into rings.

2 Heat the oil in a heavy-based saucepan, add the vegetables and cook for *5 minutes*. Add the bacon and continue cooking for a few minutes. Add the stock and split peas. Season well with salt and pepper and the mixed herbs. Simmer gently for *1 hour*. Blend the soup in a liquidizer until smooth.

3 Return the soup to the saucepan and warm over a low heat. Stir in the cream. Pour into warmed individual soup bowls and garnish each serving with chopped parsley.

Preparation time: 10 minutes, plus soaking
Cooking time: about 1¼ hours
Serves 6

1 Toast the peanuts in a dry frying pan, stirring continuously, until golden. Allow to cool a little, then roughly chop. Heat the oil and fry the onions until golden brown. Add the garlic, chillies, peanuts, reserving some to garnish, ground coriander, cumin and turmeric and fry for *2–3 minutes* or until the spices have cooked through and released a strong aroma.

2 Stir the coconut milk into the spice mixture, cover the pan and leave to simmer for *15 minutes*. Season the spiced coconut with salt, pepper and sugar to taste. Add the shredded chicken and half of the bean sprouts to the coconut mixture and simmer for *5 minutes*.

3 Meanwhile, blanch the fresh noodles in boiling water and divide between 4 large bowls. Sprinkle with the spring onions and chopped coriander and divide the remaining raw bean sprouts between the bowls.

4 Ladle the chicken and coconut mixture over the noodles and serve with chopped spring onions, red chilli and the reserved toasted peanuts.

Preparation time: 20 minutes
Cooking time: 28–30 minutes
Serves 4

Laksa

This rich and creamy coconut dish is very filling. It is made with fine bean thread vermicelli in the Philippines and flat rice noodles in Malaysia.

125 g (4 oz) roasted peanuts, skinned
3 tablespoons groundnut oil
2 large onions, finely chopped
4 garlic cloves, crushed
3 red bird's eye chillies, finely chopped
1 tablespoon ground coriander
1 tablespoon ground cumin
2 teaspoons ground turmeric
1.2 litres (2 pints) coconut milk
1–2 tablespoons sugar, to taste

375 g (12 oz) cooked chicken, shredded
175 g (6 oz) bean sprouts
500 g (1 lb) fresh flat rice noodles
4 spring onions, chopped
3 tablespoons chopped fresh coriander leaves
salt and pepper
TO SERVE:
spring onions, chopped
1 large red chilli, finely sliced

White Fish Chowder

2 rindless bacon rashers
500 g (1 lb) coley, haddock or
  cod
50 g (2 oz) butter or margarine
4 medium potatoes, diced
2 leeks, sliced into rings
50 g (2 oz) button mushrooms
600 ml (1 pint) milk
pinch of grated nutmeg
250 g (8 oz) can tomatoes
salt and pepper
1 tablespoon chopped
  parsley, to garnish

1 Dice the bacon and fry in its own fat until crisp; remove from the pan. Cut the fish into small pieces, removing skin and bones.

2 Heat the butter or margarine in a saucepan, then add the fish, potatoes, leeks and mushrooms. Cook for *2 minutes*. Add the milk, then simmer gently for *15–20 minutes*. Season with salt and pepper, to taste, and the nutmeg. Stir in the bacon and tomatoes and heat through gently.

3 Pour the chowder into warmed individual soup bowls and garnish with the chopped parsley.

Preparation time: 10 minutes
Cooking time: 30–35 minutes
Serves 6

Cook's Tip
Frozen cod steaks are ideal for this chowder. Defrost for about *15 minutes*, then cut them into cubes and cook while they are still partially frozen.

Eight Treasure Soup

The name 'eight treasure' refers to the eight special ingredients used in this soup. In China, the number eight is regarded as providing complete balance and harmony, and eight treasure dishes are made on special occasions.

1.2 litres (2 pints) Chicken
  Stock (see page 9) or water
50 g (2 oz) frozen peas
50 g (2 oz) frozen sweetcorn
  kernels
100 g (3½ oz) boneless,
  skinless chicken breast, cut
  into very thin strips
75 g (3 oz) fresh shiitake
  mushrooms, very thinly
  sliced, with stalks removed
3 tablespoons soy sauce
2 tablespoons rice wine or dry
  sherry
1 tablespoon cornflour
50 g (2 oz) cooked peeled
  prawns, thawed and dried
  thoroughly if frozen
50 g (2 oz) cooked ham, thinly
  sliced
150 g (5 oz) firm bean curd
  (tofu), drained and thinly
  sliced
50 g (2 oz) baby spinach,
  trimmed and very finely
  shredded
salt and pepper

1 Bring the stock or water to the boil in a large saucepan. Add the frozen peas and sweetcorn and simmer for *3 minutes*. Add the chicken, mushrooms, soy sauce and rice wine or sherry. Stir well and simmer for *3 minutes*.

2 Blend the cornflour to a paste with a little cold water, then pour it into the soup and stir to mix. Simmer, stirring, for *1–2 minutes* until the soup thickens.

3 Turn the heat down to low and add the prawns, ham, bean curd and spinach. Simmer for about *2 minutes* until the spinach is just wilted, stirring once or twice. Take care to stir gently so that the bean curd does not break up. Taste and add salt and pepper, plus more soy sauce, if liked. Serve hot.

Preparation time: 15–20 minutes
Cooking time: about 15 minutes
Serves 4–6

Borscht

500 g (1 lb) raw beetroot
2 carrots
1 onion
1.2 litres (2 pints) Beef
    Stock (see page 9)

1 bay leaf
salt and pepper
150 ml (¼ pint) natural
    yogurt, to garnish

1 Grate or finely chop the beetroot. Finely chop one carrot and the onion. Grate the second carrot. Put the vegetables, stock and bay leaf into a saucepan and season with salt and pepper. Bring to the boil, reduce the heat and simmer for *1 hour*. Taste the soup and adjust the seasoning, if necessary.

2 Pour the borscht into warmed individual soup bowls and garnish each serving with a spoonful of yogurt.

Preparation time: 10 minutes
Cooking time: 1 hour
Serves 6

Variation
To make traditional borscht, add 250 g (8 oz) cubed lean beef to the soup at the start of cooking. About *15 minutes* before the end of the cooking time, add 125 g (4 oz) shredded cabbage to the soup and continue to cook until all the vegetables are tender.

Bean Soup

375 g (12 oz) dried haricot
    beans
1 carrot, chopped
1 onion, quartered
1 bouquet garni
125 g (4 oz) cooked smoked
    ham, cubed

40 g (1½ oz) butter
2 shallots, finely chopped
1 garlic clove, crushed
1 tablespoon chopped parsley
salt and pepper
125 g (4 oz) croûtons,
    to serve

1 Soak the beans overnight in cold water and drain.

2 Place the beans in a large pan with 2 litres (3½ pints) water and bring to the boil over a medium heat. Boil for *1½ hours* or until the beans are just tender. Add the carrot, onion, bouquet garni and the cubed ham and simmer for *20–30 minutes*. Remove the bouquet garni and place the soup in a blender or food processor. Purée until smooth. Return the purée to the pan and reheat over a medium heat.

3 Melt the butter in a heavy-based pan and gently fry the chopped shallots and garlic until golden but not brown. Add the chopped parsley and mix together very quickly. Add the shallot mixture to the bean purée.

4 Mix well with a wooden spoon, season generously with salt and pepper, then pour into warmed individual soup bowls. Sprinkle with croûtons and serve hot.

Preparation time: 30 minutes, plus soaking
Cooking time: 2½ hours
Serves 4

French Onion Soup

50 g (2 oz) butter
750 g (1½ lb) onions, thinly sliced
2 teaspoons sugar
2 teaspoons plain flour
1.2 litres (2 pints) Beef Stock (see page 9)

½ French bread stick, sliced
25 g (1 oz) grated Gruyère cheese
salt and pepper

1 Melt the butter in a large saucepan and add the onions and sugar. Lower the heat to a bare simmer and cook the onions very slowly for *20–30 minutes* until they are soft and a really deep golden brown. Stir occasionally and take care that they cook to a good colour without burning.

2 Stir the flour into the onion mixture and cook over a very low heat for about *5 minutes*, stirring well to prevent it burning or sticking to the bottom of the pan.

3 Add the beef stock and the salt and pepper. Turn up the heat and bring to the boil, stirring. Reduce the heat and simmer for *15–20 minutes*. Taste the soup and add more salt and pepper, if necessary.

4 Meanwhile, toast the slices of French bread lightly on both sides. Sprinkle with the grated cheese. Pour the soup into a hot tureen. Place a piece of toast in each serving bowl and ladle the hot soup around the bread.

Preparation time: 30 minutes
Cooking time: 1 hour
Serves 4–5

Purée of Potato Soup with Bacon and Chives

50 g (2 oz) butter
1 large onion, roughly chopped
750 g (1½ lb) potatoes, roughly chopped
750 ml (1¼ pints) Chicken Stock (see page 9)
750 ml (1¼ pints) milk

50 ml (2 fl oz) single cream
6 rindless streaky bacon rashers, chopped and crisply fried
salt and pepper
1 tablespoon snipped chives, to garnish

1 Melt the butter in a large saucepan and fry the onion until just softened. Add the potatoes, stock and milk and season with salt and pepper. Bring to the boil, then reduce the heat and simmer for *40–45 minutes*, stirring occasionally to prevent the potatoes from sticking.

2 Purée the soup in a liquidizer or food processor until smooth. Return to the pan, taste and adjust the seasoning, if necessary, and stir in the cream and bacon. Bring to the boil and serve in warmed individual soup bowls, garnished with snipped chives.

Preparation time: 15–20 minutes
Cooking time: about 1 hour
Serves 6–8

Noodle Soup with Marinated Chicken

This soup is without doubt Burma's most common dish. In this version, chicken replaces the fish which is its usual basic ingredient.

300 g (10 oz) boneless, skinless chicken breasts
1 teaspoon turmeric
2 teaspoons salt
3 tablespoons peanuts, skinned
2 lemon grass stalks
3 tablespoons white long-grain rice
2 tablespoons vegetable oil
1 onion, chopped
3 garlic cloves, crushed
5 cm (2 inch) piece of fresh root ginger, peeled and finely chopped

¼ teaspoon paprika
2 red bird's eye chillies, chopped
2–3 tablespoons fish sauce (nam pla)
900 ml (1½ pints) water
250 g (8 oz) wheat noodles
TO SERVE:
3 hard-boiled eggs, halved
2 tablespoons chopped fresh coriander leaves
3 spring onions, finely chopped
crushed dried chilli

1 Cut the chicken breasts into 2.5 cm (1 inch) cubes. Mix the turmeric with the salt and rub the mixture into the cubes of chicken. Leave to stand for *30 minutes*.

2 Meanwhile, toast the peanuts in a dry frying pan, stirring continuously, until golden. Allow to cool. Bruise the lemon grass with the side of a rolling pin to release the flavour. Finely crush the roasted peanuts in a food processor or using a pestle and mortar. Heat a dry frying pan and toast the rice until golden brown, then finely crush it to a powder in a food processor or spice grinder.

3 Heat the oil in a large pan and fry the onion until just softened. Add the marinated chicken together with the garlic, ginger, lemon grass, paprika and chillies. Add the fish sauce and water and bring to the boil.

4 Reduce the heat to simmering, mix the crushed peanuts and ground rice together and add to the pan. Simmer for about *10–15 minutes,* or until the chicken has cooked through and the broth thickened slightly.

5 Meanwhile, bring a pan of water to the boil, add the wheat noodles and cook for *3–4 minutes,* or until just done. Drain and refresh with cold water and then divide them between large soup bowls.

6 Ladle the chicken soup over the noodles and serve topped with the hard-boiled eggs, chopped coriander and spring onions. Add an extra splash of fish sauce and a sprinkling of crushed dried chilli, to taste. Eat the soup with a spoon and fork.

Preparation time: 20 minutes, plus standing
Cooking time: about 35 minutes
Serves 4–6

Stews and Casseroles

A hearty stew can be very simple to prepare and extremely nutritious to eat. Any number of different ingredients can be included in a stew or casserole including vegetables, fish, poultry and meat. These are perfect recipes for easy eating, and they are especially warming on cold winter evenings.

Fish Cassoulet

175 g (6 oz) dried haricot
  beans, soaked overnight
2 tablespoons olive oil
50 g (2 oz) bacon, diced
2 garlic cloves, chopped
1 onion, sliced
1 leek, sliced
125 g (4 oz) halibut, filleted
  and skinned
250 g (8 oz) coley, filleted and
  skinned
1 small mackerel, filleted and
  skinned
3 large tomatoes, skinned and
  chopped
1 bay leaf
150 ml (¼ pint) dry white wine
salt and pepper

1 Boil the beans in the water in which they have soaked for
1–1½ hours, until tender. (Do not add salt as this tends to make
them hard.) Drain and set aside.

2 Heat the oil and fry the bacon, garlic, onion and leek for
5–8 minutes over a moderate heat, until just softened.

3 Cut the fish into bite-sized pieces, discarding all the bones.
Layer with the fried vegetables, bacon and chopped tomatoes in
a large casserole dish, and season with salt and pepper. Add the
bay leaf and pour on the white wine.

4 Cover the casserole and bake in a preheated oven, 180°C
(350°F), Gas Mark 4, for about *1 hour* until heated through.
Remove the bay leaf before serving.

Preparation time: 25 minutes, plus soaking
Cooking time: 2–2½ hours
Serves 4

Smoked Cod Stew with Raisins and Marsala

This stew is based on a Sicilian dish which uses salt
cod. This version uses smoked cod instead.

50 g (2 oz) raisins
3 tablespoons Marsala
4 tablespoons olive oil
250 g (8 oz) baby onions,
  halved if large
2 garlic cloves, chopped
1 tablespoon chopped sage
4 large beef tomatoes,
  skinned and chopped
150 ml (¼ pint) Vegetable
  Stock (see page 9)
2 tablespoons balsamic
  vinegar
500 g (1 lb) skinless undyed
  smoked cod fillet, washed,
  dried and cut into bite-
  sized pieces
25 g (1 oz) black olives, pitted
25 g (1 oz) pine nuts, toasted
salt and pepper
2 tablespoons chopped
  parsley

1 Place the raisins in a small bowl, pour over the Marsala and
allow to soak for *1 hour* until the raisins are plump. Strain and
reserve the raisins and Marsala.

2 Heat the oil in a large saucepan and fry the baby onions for
15 minutes over a medium heat until golden and caramelized.
Add the garlic and sage and fry for a further *5 minutes*. Add the
tomatoes, stir-fry for *3 minutes* and then stir in the vegetable
stock, vinegar and reserved Marsala. Bring to the boil, cover and
simmer gently for *30 minutes*.

3 Add the fish to the stew with the raisins, olives and pine nuts
and simmer gently for *4–5 minutes* until the fish is cooked.
Season with salt and pepper, to taste. Sprinkle over the parsley
and serve immediately.

Preparation time: 15 minutes, plus soaking
Cooking time: about 1 hour
Serves 4

Turkey and Chestnut Casserole

1.25 kg (2½ lb) boneless raw
turkey meat, skinned and
cubed
2 tablespoons vegetable oil
50 g (2 oz) butter
1 onion, sliced
1 garlic clove, chopped
125 g (4 oz) button
mushrooms
40 g (1½ oz) plain flour
150 ml (¼ pint) turkey or
Chicken Stock
(see page 9)
2 tablespoons cranberry jelly
250 g (8 oz) cooked peeled
chestnuts

salt and pepper
fresh parsley, to
garnish (optional)
MARINADE:
600 ml (1 pint) dry white wine
50 ml (2 fl oz) white wine
vinegar
1 onion, sliced
1 garlic clove, chopped
2 tablespoons thyme
1 bay leaf
1 lemon slice
salt
12 black peppercorns,
crushed

1 Combine all the ingredients for the marinade in a large casserole. Add the turkey to the dish, cover and chill overnight. Lift the turkey from the marinade and set aside. Strain the marinade and reserve. Heat the oil in a heavy-based pan and brown the turkey. Place in a large flameproof casserole.

2 Melt the butter in the pan and cook the onion and garlic, stirring, for *5 minutes*. Add the mushrooms to the pan and cook for *5 minutes*. Blend the flour into the pan. Cook, stirring, for *2–3 minutes*. Gradually whisk in the reserved marinade and stock. Bring to the boil, stirring constantly. Remove from the heat and add the cranberry jelly, salt and pepper. Pour the sauce over the turkey pieces, cover and cook in a preheated oven, 180°C (350°F), Gas Mark 4, for *1 hour*.

3 Transfer the turkey, mushrooms and onions to a dish and keep warm. Place the casserole on the hob, bring to the boil and reduce by a third. Add the chestnuts and simmer for *15 minutes*. Coat the turkey with the sauce and garnish with parsley, if liked.

Preparation time: 40 minutes, plus marinating
Cooking time: 2 hours
Serves 4

Turkey Mexicana

50 g (2 oz) seasoned plain
flour
4 turkey fillets
3 tablespoons vegetable oil
1 onion, thinly sliced
1 small red pepper, cored,
deseeded and sliced
300 ml (½ pint) Chicken Stock
(see page 9)
25 g (1 oz) seedless raisins
pinch of ground cloves
pinch of ground cumin

½ teaspoon ground cinnamon
3 tomatoes, skinned,
deseeded and sliced
1 teaspoon chilli powder
1 teaspoon sesame seeds
25 g (1 oz) plain chocolate,
grated
salt and pepper
TO GARNISH:
lime or lemon wedges
coriander sprigs

1 Use the seasoned flour to coat the turkey fillets. Heat the oil in a frying pan and brown the turkey. Transfer to a casserole.

2 Add the onion and red pepper to the frying pan and cook gently until softened. Sprinkle in any remaining seasoned flour and cook for *2–3 minutes*. Stir in the stock, raisins, cloves, cumin, cinnamon, tomatoes, chilli powder, sesame seeds and chocolate. Bring to the boil and simmer for *10 minutes*.

3 Pour the sauce over the turkey. Cover the casserole and cook in a preheated oven, 160°C (325°F), Gas Mark 3, for *50 minutes*. Adjust the seasoning, if necessary, and serve, garnished with the lime or lemon wedges.

Preparation time: 20 minutes
Cooking time: 1¼ hours
Serves 4

1 Place the saffron in a small bowl and pour over the boiling water. Leave to infuse for *10 minutes*.

2 Melt the butter in a large flameproof casserole, add the shallots or onion and garlic and cook, without browning, for *5–6 minutes* until softened. Add the pancetta or bacon and cook for a further *1–2 minutes*. Add the peas, lettuce, 1 teaspoon of caster sugar and the saffron and its water. Cover the casserole and cook for *10–15 minutes* until the peas are tender. If using frozen peas, add to the pan after *5 minutes*. Season with salt and pepper, to taste, and more sugar, if necessary.

3 Meanwhile, make the breadcrumb topping. Melt the butter in a frying pan, add the breadcrumbs and cook, stirring frequently, until golden brown. Remove from the heat, leave to cool slightly, then stir in the grated cheese.

4 Beat the egg yolks in a small bowl and, when the peas are cooked, ladle out 100 ml (3½ fl oz) of liquid from the casserole and whisk into the yolks. Pour back into the casserole and stir until the sauce has thickened; do not allow it to boil or it will curdle. Stir in the mint and serve sprinkled with the breadcrumb topping.

Preparation time: 20 minutes
Cooking time: 30–40 minutes
Serves 4

Green Pea Stew with Saffron and Mint

pinch of saffron threads
300 ml (½ pint) boiling water
50 g (2 oz) butter
2 shallots or 1 small onion, finely chopped
1 garlic clove, crushed
75 g (3 oz) rindless pancetta or streaky bacon, cut into strips
500 g (1 lb) shelled peas, thawed if frozen
2 little gem lettuces, cut into wide strips
1–2 teaspoons caster sugar
2 egg yolks, beaten
2 tablespoons chopped mint
salt and pepper

TOPPING:
25 g (1 oz) butter
75 g (3 oz) fresh white breadcrumbs
25 g (1 oz) Parmesan or Pecorino cheese, finely grated

Pork and Dumplings

25 g (1 oz) butter or margarine
625 g (1¼ lb) lean boneless
    pork, cut into cubes
2 onions, chopped
125 g (4 oz) no-need-to-soak
    dried apricots
25 g (1 oz) plain flour
600 ml (1 pint) Chicken Stock
    (see page 9)
300 ml (½ pint) dry cider

salt and pepper
DUMPLINGS:
125 g (4 oz) self-raising flour
1 tablespoon chopped parsley
50 g (2 oz) suet
2 tablespoons water
TO GARNISH:
halved orange slices
rosemary sprigs

1 Heat the butter in a heavy-based frying pan and fry the pork until golden, then transfer it to a casserole. Cook the onions in the remaining fat until soft and add to the casserole with the apricots. Sprinkle over the flour, then pour in the stock and cider. Mix all the ingredients together, season, cover, and cook in a preheated oven, 180°C (350°F), Gas Mark 4, for *2 hours*.

2 To make the dumplings, sift the flour and a pinch of salt into a bowl, add the parsley and suet and mix well. Stir in the water and blend to make a soft dough. Divide the dough into 8 pieces and roll into small balls on a lightly floured surface. Add the dumplings to the casserole and cook for a further *30 minutes*, or until the dumplings are cooked. Serve the casserole garnished with the halved orange slices and rosemary sprigs.

Preparation time: 20 minutes
Cooking time: 2¾ hours
Serves 4

Cook's Tip
A flameproof casserole is useful for this type of dish. All the ingredients can be browned and cooked in the one pan.

Milanese Stew with Sausages

This hearty casserole is full of juicy, meaty flavour. Eat it with plenty of crusty bread to mop up the sauce.

300 g (10 oz) pork rind
25 g (1 oz) butter
3–4 tablespoons olive oil
2 large onions, sliced
2 large carrots, sliced
2 celery sticks, chopped
625 g (1¼ lb) boneless pork,
    diced
150 ml (¼ pint) dry white wine

1.5 litres (2½ pints) Chicken
    Stock (see page 9)
250 g (8 oz) Italian pork
    sausage or Continental
    sausage, cut into 2.5 cm
    (1 inch) slices
750 g (1½ lb) Savoy cabbage,
    trimmed and shredded
salt and pepper

1 Place the pork rind in a pan, cover with water and salt lightly. Bring to the boil and cook for *10 minutes*. Drain and cut the rind into 5 cm x 1 cm (2 inch x ½ inch) strips.

2 Heat the butter and half the oil in another pan. Cook the onions until soft but not brown, then add the carrots and celery, and cook for about *5 minutes*, stirring frequently.

3 Take the vegetables from the pan. Heat the remaining oil and cook the pork until it is well sealed. Return the vegetables and pork rind to the pan and pour on the white wine and stock. Season to taste with salt and pepper.

4 Simmer gently for *1½–2 hours* until the meat is almost tender. Add the sausage and cabbage, and continue cooking for a further *25–30 minutes*. Taste and adjust the seasoning, and transfer to a serving dish. Serve hot.

Preparation time: 20–25 minutes
Cooking time: 2½–3 hours
Serves 4–6

Cook's Tip
Make this dish the day before you eat it, as standing improves the flavour. Refrigerate it when cold and reheat for *40 minutes* over a low heat the following day.

Braised Pork with Artichoke Hearts

75 g (3 oz) butter
500 g (1 lb) pork fillet, cut into 1 cm (½ inch) pieces
1 small onion, thinly sliced
1 garlic clove, crushed
50 g (2 oz) button mushrooms, sliced
1 teaspoon dried rosemary, crumbled
200 ml (7 fl oz) dry white wine or cider
425 g (14 oz) can artichoke hearts, drained and halved
1 teaspoon plain flour
4 tablespoons double cream
salt and pepper
TO GARNISH:
strips of lemon rind
chopped parsley

1 Melt 25 g (1 oz) of the butter in a heavy-based frying pan, add the pork and fry briskly, turning, to brown and seal. Transfer to a flameproof casserole.

2 Melt half the remaining butter in the pan, add the onion and fry for *2 minutes*. Add the garlic and mushrooms, stir well and fry for a further *2 minutes*. Transfer to the casserole. Add the rosemary, wine and artichoke hearts to the pan, bring to the boil and season with salt and pepper, to taste. Pour into the casserole. Transfer to a preheated oven, 160°C (325°F), Gas Mark 3, and cook for *30 minutes*, or until tender.

3 Beat together the flour and the remaining butter. Remove the casserole from the oven, whisk in the paste gradually and bring to the boil on top of the hob. Simmer for *2–3 minutes*, stirring. Stir in the cream and heat through without boiling. Taste for seasoning and adjust, if necessary, then serve garnished with lemon rind and parsley.

Preparation time: 15 minutes
Cooking time: about 1 hour
Serves 4

Hungarian Goulash

25 g (1 oz) plain flour
¼ teaspoon mustard powder
1 tablespoon paprika
625 g (1¼ lb) stewing or braising steak, cut into cubes
3 tablespoons oil
2 onions, sliced into rings
1 red pepper, cored, deseeded and sliced
1 green pepper, cored, deseeded and sliced
500 g (1 lb) tomatoes, peeled and quartered
600 ml (1 pint) Beef Stock (see page 9)
150 ml (¼ pint) soured cream
salt and pepper
1 tablespoon chopped parsley, to garnish

1 Mix together the flour, mustard and paprika, season with salt and pepper and toss the meat cubes in the mixture. Heat the oil in a frying pan and cook the meat until brown on all sides. Transfer to a casserole. Gently fry the onions and peppers in the remaining fat until soft, and add to the casserole with the tomatoes and beef stock.

2 Mix the ingredients together well. Cover the casserole and cook in a preheated oven, 160°C (325°F), Gas Mark 3, for *2–2½ hours* or until the meat is tender.

3 Pour the soured cream over the meat and serve immediately, garnished with chopped parsley.

Preparation time: 15 minutes
Cooking time: 2½–3 hours
Serves 4

Irish Stew

One of Ireland's most famous dishes, this is traditionally made with mutton, but nowadays, since mutton is rarely available, lamb chops from the neck or shoulder, or stewing lamb, baked off the bone, are used instead. Floury potatoes are essential, waxy ones will not break down into the liquid.

1 kg (2 lb) neck of lamb, cut into rings about 1.5 cm (¾ inch) thick
2 large onions, sliced
1 kg (2 lb) floury potatoes, sliced
2 large carrots, sliced
2–3 tablespoons finely chopped parsley
400 ml (14 fl oz) lamb stock or water
salt and pepper

1 Layer the meat and vegetables in a deep saucepan or flame-proof casserole. Sprinkle over half the parsley and season between each layer with salt and pepper; finish with a layer of potatoes. Pour over the stock or water and cover tightly with a piece of buttered greaseproof paper. Cover this with foil and a tightly fitting lid.

2 Bring to the boil, then reduce the heat and simmer very gently for *1½–2 hours* either on the hob or in a preheated oven, 160°C (325°F), Gas Mark 3, until the meat is tender, the liquid well absorbed and the stew rich and pulpy. To thicken the juices, remove a few potato slices, mash them and return to the pan. Add the remaining parsley, then taste and adjust the seasoning, if necessary.

Preparation time: 20 minutes
Cooking time: 1½–2 hours
Serves 4

Vegetable Casserole with Cheese Scones

1 tablespoon sunflower oil
1 onion, chopped
250 g (8 oz) white turnips, diced
250 g (8 oz) carrots, sliced
375 g (12 oz) leeks, chopped
250 g (8 oz) courgettes, sliced
400 g (13 oz) can chopped tomatoes
1 tablespoon tomato purée
150 ml (¼ pint) Vegetable Stock (see page 9)
1 teaspoon dried mixed herbs
salt and pepper
SCONES:
50 g (2 oz) butter or margarine
1 small onion, finely chopped
250 g (8 oz) self-raising flour
pinch of salt
75 g (3 oz) Double Gloucester cheese with onions and chives, finely grated
4–5 tablespoons milk

1 Heat the oil in a large saucepan and cook the onion, turnips, carrots and leeks, covered, for *10 minutes*.

2 Stir in the courgettes, chopped tomatoes, tomato purée and stock. Bring to the boil, lower the heat and simmer for *5 minutes*. Stir in the herbs, season with salt and pepper, to taste and transfer to an ovenproof casserole.

3 To make the scones, melt 15 g (½ oz) of the butter or margarine in a saucepan. Add the onion and cook for *4 minutes* until soft. Leave to cool.

4 In a mixing bowl rub the remaining butter or margarine into the flour. Add the salt. Stir in the onion and the cheese. Add enough milk to mix to a soft dough.

5 Knead the scone dough lightly on a floured surface. Pat or roll out to a thickness of 2 cm (¾ inch) and cut out rounds with a 5 cm (2 inch) scone cutter.

6 Place the scones on top of the vegetables, brush with a little milk and cook in a preheated oven, 200°C (400°F), Gas Mark 6, for *20–25 minutes* until the scones are golden. Serve the casserole immediately.

Preparation time: 15 minutes
Cooking time: 40–45 minutes
Serves 4

Fish, Meat and Poultry

A varied selection of recipes including stir-fries and curries. This chapter provides many ideas that are ideal for informal entertaining, with minimum fuss and less time spent in the kitchen.

Sweet and Sour Fish

1 egg white

2 teaspoons cornflour

pinch of salt

500 g (1 lb) cod or haddock fillets, skinned and cut into 2.5 cm (1 inch) chunks

about 600 ml (1 pint) ground-nut oil, for deep-frying

2 tablespoons finely chopped coriander, to garnish

deep-fried shredded seaweed (Chinese cabbage) to serve (optional)

SAUCE:

1 tablespoon cornflour

125 ml (4 fl oz) cold fish stock or water

1 tablespoon soy sauce

1 tablespoon rice wine or dry sherry

1 tablespoon rice wine vinegar or white wine or cider vinegar

1 tablespoon dark or light soft, brown sugar

1 tablespoon tomato purée

1 Lightly beat the egg white in a shallow dish with the cornflour and salt. Add the chunks of fish and turn gently to coat. Set aside.

2 Prepare the sauce. Blend the cornflour in a jug with 2 table-spoons of the stock or water, then add the remaining stock or water and the remaining sauce ingredients. Stir well to combine.

3 Heat the oil in a wok or deep frying pan until very hot but not smoking. Deep-fry the fish chunks a few at a time for *2–3 minutes* per batch until golden. Lift out the fish with a slotted spoon and drain on kitchen paper while deep-frying the remainder.

4 Very carefully pour off all the oil from the pan and wipe it clean with kitchen paper. Pour the sauce mixture into the pan and bring to the boil over a high heat, stirring constantly, until thickened and glossy. Lower the heat, add the fish and simmer gently for *30–60 seconds* until heated through. Garnish with finely chopped coriander and serve immediately, accompanied by deep-fried shredded seaweed, if liked.

Preparation time: 10–15 minutes
Cooking time: 10–15 minutes
Serves 4

Moules Marinières

50 g (2 oz) butter, softened

6 shallots or small onions, finely chopped

1 bouquet garni

450 ml (¾ pint) dry white wine

3 kg (6 lb) or (3.6 litres/ 6 pints) fresh mussels, scrubbed

25 g (1 oz) plain flour

salt and pepper

chopped parsley, to garnish

1 Melt half the butter in a pan, add the shallots or onions and fry gently until golden. Add the bouquet garni, wine and salt and pepper to taste. Bring to the boil. Discard any open mussels. Put the closed mussels into the boiling liquid. Cover and simmer for about *5 minutes* until the mussels' shells have opened. Remove the mussels from the pan with a slotted spoon, discarding any that have not opened. Pile the mussels into a warmed serving dish and keep hot.

2 Bring the sauce in the pan to the boil and boil until reduced by half. Remove the bouquet garni.

3 Blend the remaining butter with the flour, divide into small pieces and add gradually to the stock, stirring continually, until melted. Bring to the boil, stirring, then simmer for *2 minutes*. Pour over the mussels and garnish with parsley.

Preparation time: 25 minutes
Cooking time: about 20 minutes
Serves 6

Crunchy Fish Bake

50 g (2 oz) butter or margarine	salt and pepper
50 g (2 oz) plain flour	TOPPING:
600 ml (1 pint) milk	175 g (6 oz) wholemeal flour
¼ teaspoon dill weed	50 g (2 oz) oatmeal
200 g (7 oz) can tuna, drained and flaked	125 g (4 oz) butter
	salt and pepper
125 g (4 oz) cooked peeled prawns	TO GARNISH:
	2 whole cooked prawns
2 tablespoons lemon juice	parsley sprigs

1 Melt the butter or margarine over a low heat, stir in the flour and cook for *2 minutes*, then gradually add the milk, stirring all the time. Bring the sauce to the boil and simmer gently for a few minutes. Add the dill weed, tuna, prawns, lemon juice and salt and pepper, to taste. Pour into an ovenproof dish.

2 To make the topping, place the flour, oatmeal, butter and salt and pepper in a bowl. Using your fingertips, rub the fat into the dry ingredients until the mixture resembles fine breadcrumbs.

3 Spoon the topping over the fish mixture and bake in a preheated oven, 190°C (375°F), Gas Mark 5, for *30–40 minutes*. Serve hot, garnished with whole prawns and parsley.

Preparation time: 15–20 minutes
Cooking time: 40–50 minutes
Serves 4

Breton Tuna

140 g (4½ oz) butter	1 small cauliflower
2 large onions, chopped	500 g (1 lb) small new potatoes (unpeeled)
1.5 kg (3 lb) tuna	
2–3 garlic cloves, chopped	salt and pepper
4 tomatoes, quartered	TO GARNISH:
500 ml (17 fl oz) dry white wine	1½ tablespoons chopped parsley
1 thyme sprig	
1 parsley sprig	1½ tablespoons chopped chives
1 bay leaf	

1 Heat the butter in a large flameproof casserole and fry the onions over a moderate heat for *5 minutes* until soft and just beginning to brown. Add the tuna, season with salt and pepper and leave to brown gently, turning from time to time.

2 Add the garlic and tomatoes to the casserole. Pour on the white wine, bring to the boil and add the herbs. Cover and simmer over a low heat for *1 hour*. Remove the bay leaf.

3 Lift the tuna out of the casserole with a slotted spoon and keep warm. Divide the cauliflower into florets and add them to the casserole with the potatoes. Simmer gently for *20–30 minutes,* until tender.

4 Cut the fish into serving pieces and remove any skin and bones. Arrange on a serving dish, spoon on the sauce, cauliflower and potatoes and garnish with parsley and chives.

Preparation time: 10 minutes
Cooking time: about 1¾ hours
Serves 6

Smoked Fish Pie

500 g (1 lb) smoked haddock
450 ml (¾ pint) milk
50 g (2 oz) butter
1 onion, finely chopped
175 g (6 oz) mushrooms, sliced
25 g (1 oz) plain flour
1 teaspoon prepared English
    mustard
2 tablespoons finely chopped
    parsley
1 tablespoon lemon juice

2–3 eggs, hard-boiled and
    roughly chopped
salt and pepper
TOPPING:
875 g (1¾ lb) potatoes, cooked
    and mashed
25 g (1 oz) butter, melted
3–4 tablespoons milk
50 g (2 oz) Cheddar cheese,
    grated

1 Put the haddock in a shallow saucepan, pour on the milk, heat slowly until simmering and cook for *5–10 minutes*.

2 Meanwhile, melt the butter in a separate saucepan and fry the onion until soft but not brown. Add the mushrooms and continue to fry until colouring. Stir in the flour and cook gently for about *1 minute*, then remove from the heat.

3 When the fish is cooked, strain the liquid into a jug and gradually add to the onion and mushroom mixture, stirring well. Bring to the boil and simmer for *10 minutes* until thick, stirring continually. Add the mustard, parsley, lemon juice and eggs and season with salt and pepper, to taste. Flake the fish, remove the bones and add to the sauce. Pile into a deep ovenproof dish.

4 To make the topping, mix the potatoes with the melted butter and milk, season well and pile roughly on top of the fish mixture, covering it evenly. Scatter over the cheese and bake in a pre-heated oven, 190°C (375°F), Gas Mark 5, for about *30 minutes*, until piping hot and crisp.

Preparation time: 20–30 minutes
Cooking time: about 50 minutes
Serves 4–6

Cook's Tip
When using smoked fish in this or any other recipe, buy naturally smoked, undyed fish. The best quality smoked haddock is Finnan haddock. For extra flavour add 6 pepper-corns, a blade of mace, 1 bay leaf, 1 wedge of onion and 2 cloves to the milk, while cooking the fish.

Seafood Creole

4 tablespoons olive oil
2 onions, chopped
2 green peppers, cored,
    deseeded and chopped
2 garlic cloves, crushed
500 g (1 lb) mixed seafood
    (e.g. cooked lobster meat,
    large prawns, crab meat)
4 tablespoons white wine
salt and pepper

coriander sprigs, to garnish
SOFRITO:
3 tablespoons olive oil
1 onion, chopped
3 garlic cloves, crushed
500 g (1 lb) tomatoes, skinned
    and chopped
1 tablespoon chopped
    coriander
salt and pepper

1 First make the *sofrito* (a basic Spanish tomato sauce). Heat the olive oil in a saucepan and add the onion and garlic. Fry over a gentle heat until soft and translucent. Add the tomatoes and coriander, and season with salt and pepper. Simmer over a very low heat for *20–30 minutes*, until thickened.

2 In a large frying pan, heat the olive oil and fry the onions, green peppers and garlic until softened and golden. Stir occasionally and do not allow them to brown.

3 Prepare the seafood, removing any shells from the lobster, prawns or crab meat. Add to the vegetables in the pan with the prepared *sofrito*. Simmer gently for *15 minutes*.

4 Add the wine and stir well. Continue cooking for *15 minutes*. Taste and adjust the seasoning, if necessary, and serve garnished with coriander.

Preparation time: 30 minutes
Cooking time: 1–1¼ hours
Serves 4

Chicken Fricassée

3 tablespoons olive oil

125 g (4 oz) rindless unsmoked bacon rashers, cut into strips

2 onions, thinly sliced

2 carrots, cut into 5 cm (2 inch) barrel-shaped pieces

2 x 1 kg (2 lb) chickens, jointed into 6 pieces

75 g (3 oz) butter

2 tablespoons plain flour

4 tablespoons brandy

150 ml (¼ pint) dry white wine

900 ml (1½ pints) Chicken Stock, plus 4 tablespoons (see page 9)

1 tablespoon chopped thyme

2 teaspoons finely chopped parsley

1 bay leaf, crumbled

4 large potatoes, cubed

1.2 litres (2 pints) cold water

250 g (8 oz) small button mushrooms, stems trimmed

2 tablespoons cornflour

salt and pepper

1 Heat 1 tablespoon of the oil in a large frying pan. Add the bacon and cook for *5–10 minutes*. Remove and drain on kitchen paper. Cook the onions and carrots in the pan for *20 minutes*. Remove from the pan with a slotted spoon and set aside.

2 Season the chicken pieces with salt and pepper. Heat the remaining oil and 25 g (1 oz) of the butter in the frying pan. Add the chicken and cook for *10 minutes,* until lightly browned. Sprinkle over the flour and cook for *2–3 minutes,* turning occasionally until the flour has browned. Return the onions and carrots to the pan.

3 Warm the brandy in a flameproof ladle and pour over the chicken pieces. Carefully set alight. If the flames become too vigorous, cover the pan with a tight lid. When the flames have died, put the chicken in a large flameproof casserole. Add the wine to the frying pan, increase the heat to high and bring to the boil. Blend in 900 ml (1½ pints) of the chicken stock, the thyme, parsley and bay leaf and bring to a simmer. Pour the sauce over the chicken. Cover and cook in a preheated oven, 180°C (350°F), Gas Mark 4, for *45 minutes*.

4 Bring the potato cubes and water to the boil in a saucepan. Drain the potatoes. Melt 25 g (1 oz) of the butter in a frying pan. Add the mushrooms and cook for *5 minutes*, stirring constantly. Remove and set aside.

5 Transfer the cooked chicken to a clean flameproof casserole. Strain the vegetables and sauce through a sieve into a frying pan. Add the vegetables to the chicken pieces and keep warm.

6 Bring the sauce to the boil over a high heat. Reduce the heat and remove any fat with a spoon. Mix together the cornflour and 4 tablespoons of chicken stock and stir into the sauce. Bring to the boil and cook for *2–3 minutes*. Blend the sauce into the casserole and stir in the mushrooms. Place the casserole over a moderate heat and bring to a simmer. Cook for *20 minutes*, until heated through.

7 Meanwhile, heat the remaining butter and oil in a large frying pan, add the potatoes and fry until brown. Lower the heat and add the bacon. Cook for *1 minute* further, then scatter over the casserole.

Preparation time: 45 minutes
Cooking time: about 2½ hours
Serves 6

Beef with Broccoli and Oyster Sauce

375 g (12 oz) rump steak, in 1 piece, trimmed of all fat
1 egg white
2 tablespoons soy sauce
2 garlic cloves, crushed
2.5 cm (1 inch) piece of fresh root ginger, peeled and grated
1 tablespoon cornflour
1 teaspoon sugar
about 175 ml (6 fl oz) ground-nut oil, for frying

250 g (8 oz) broccoli, divided into small florets
125 ml (4 fl oz) rice wine or dry sherry
3 tablespoons oyster sauce
2 tablespoons soy sauce, or more to taste
salt and pepper
TO GARNISH:
sesame oil
2 tablespoons toasted sesame seeds

1 Wrap the beef in clingfilm and place it in the freezer for *1–2 hours* until it is just hard.

2 Remove the beef from the freezer and unwrap it, then slice it into small rectangles. Whisk the egg white in a bowl, add the soy sauce, garlic, ginger, cornflour and sugar and whisk to mix. Add the beef, stir to coat, then leave to marinate at room temperature for about *30 minutes* or until the beef has completely thawed.

3 Heat the oil in a deep frying pan or wok until very hot but not smoking. Add about one-third of the beef rectangles and stir them so they separate. Fry for *30–60 seconds* until the beef changes colour on all sides, lift out with a slotted spoon and drain on kitchen paper. Repeat with the remaining beef. Carefully pour off all but about 2 tablespoons of the hot oil from the pan.

4 Add the broccoli florets to the pan, sprinkle with the rice wine or sherry and toss over a moderate heat for *3 minutes*. Return the beef to the pan and add the oyster sauce and soy sauce. Increase the heat to high and stir-fry vigorously for *3–4 minutes* or until the beef and broccoli are tender. Taste and add more soy sauce, if liked. Serve hot, drizzled with sesame oil and sprinkled with sesame seeds.

Preparation time: about 15 minutes, plus freezing and marinating
Cooking time: 15–20 minutes
Serves 2–3

Stir-fried Liver with Spinach and Ginger

375 g (12 oz) lamb's liver, cut into thin triangular slices
2 tablespoons cornflour
4 tablespoons sunflower oil
500 g (1 lb) fresh spinach, washed and drained
1 teaspoon salt

2 thin slices fresh root ginger, peeled and chopped
1 tablespoon light soy sauce
1 tablespoon Chinese rice wine or dry sherry
finely chopped spring onion, to garnish

1 Blanch the slices of liver in boiling water for a few seconds. Drain and coat with cornflour.

2 Heat 2 tablespoons of the oil in a deep frying pan or wok. Add the spinach and salt and stir-fry for *2 minutes*. Remove from the pan and arrange around the edge of a warmed serving dish. Keep the spinach hot.

3 Wipe the pan clean with kitchen paper. Heat the remaining oil in the pan until very hot. Add the ginger, liver, soy sauce and wine or sherry. Stir-fry briskly for *1–2 minutes* – avoid overcooking or the liver will become tough. Pour the mixture over the spinach and garnish with spring onion.

Preparation time: 10 minutes
Cooking time: 4–5 minutes
Serves 4

Cook's Tip
Blanching liver in boiling water is a good way of ensuring that it remains tender during the cooking process. This is a robust stir-fry, quickly prepared and cooked.

1   Strip the skin and fat off the duck and discard. Cut the duck flesh into thin strips, working diagonally against the grain, then place the strips in a non-metallic dish. Mix together the marinade ingredients, pour into the dish and stir to mix. Cover and leave to marinate at room temperature for about *30 minutes*.

2   Meanwhile, cut the mango lengthways into three pieces, avoiding the stone. Peel the pieces of mango and cut the flesh into strips about the same size as the duck.

3   Heat an empty deep frying pan or wok until hot. Add half of the oil and heat until it is hot. Add half the duck strips and stir-fry over a high heat for *4–5 minutes* or until just tender. Remove the duck with a slotted spoon and repeat with the remaining oil and duck.

4   Return all of the duck to the pan and sprinkle with the chilli and rice wine or sherry. Toss to mix, then add the mango and Chinese cabbage and toss for *1–2 minutes*, just until the cabbage starts to wilt. Serve immediately.

Preparation time: 15 minutes, plus marinating
Cooking time: about 15 minutes
Serves 2–4

Stir-fried Duck with Mango

In this modern recipe the sweet, juicy fruitiness of mango counteracts the richness of duck meat and tempers the fieriness of red hot chilli.

1 large boneless duck breast (magret), weighing about 400 g (13 oz) or 2 small duck breasts
1 ripe mango
4 tablespoons groundnut oil
1 large red chilli, sliced into very thin rings
4 tablespoons Chinese rice wine or dry sherry
75 g (3 oz) Chinese cabbage or Savoy cabbage

MARINADE:
2 tablespoons light or dark soy sauce
1 tablespoon rice wine vinegar or white wine or cider vinegar
½ teaspoon chilli oil
2.5 cm (1 inch) piece of fresh root ginger, peeled and grated
½ teaspoon five-spice powder

Chicken Jalfrezi

6 tablespoons butter or ghee
1 teaspoon white cumin seeds
1 teaspoon black mustard
    seeds
2–6 garlic cloves, finely
    chopped
5 cm (2 inch) piece fresh root
    ginger, finely sliced
1 large onion, thinly sliced
750 g (1½ lb) boneless,
    skinless chicken breast,
    diced

1 tablespoon mild curry paste
½ red pepper, cored, deseeded
    and chopped
½ green pepper, cored,
    deseeded and chopped
2 tomatoes, skinned and
    chopped
1 tablespoon chopped
    coriander leaves
1–2 tablespoons water

1 Heat the butter or ghee in a large frying pan or wok. Add the cumin and mustard seeds and stir-fry for *1 minute*. Add the garlic and stir-fry for *1 minute* more. Add the ginger and stir-fry for *2 minutes*. Add the onion and stir-fry until golden – about *5 minutes*.

2 Combine the chicken pieces with the spices in the pan, stirring and turning for *5 minutes*. Add all the remaining ingredients and stir-fry for about *10 minutes*. Serve immediately.

Preparation time: 20 minutes
Cooking time: about 25 minutes
Serves 4

Variation
Chilli Chicken: This is a much hotter version of Chicken Jalfrezi. Prepare as above but add 2–10 chopped green chillies instead of the peppers. (The quantity of chillies depends on your heat threshold.)

Mughlai Beef

750 g (1½ lb) lean stewing
    steak, cubed
4 tablespoons clarified butter
    or ghee
2 garlic cloves, finely chopped
5 cm (2 inch) piece fresh root
    ginger, finely chopped
1 large onion, thinly sliced
1 tablespoon mild curry paste
50 g (2 oz) unsalted cashew
    nuts, chopped
2 tablespoons ground
    almonds

75 ml (3 fl oz) single cream
1 tablespoon chopped
    coriander
MARINADE:
75 ml (3 fl oz) natural yogurt
2 teaspoons mild curry
    powder
2 teaspoons white sugar
½ teaspoon aromatic salt
TO GARNISH:
1 tablespoon unsalted cashew
    nuts, chopped
coriander leaves

1 Combine all the marinade ingredients and mix with the stewing steak in a bowl. Cover and chill in the refrigerator for up to 24 hours.

2 Heat the butter or ghee in a large frying pan or wok. Stir-fry the garlic for *1 minute*. Add the ginger and stir-fry for *1 minute* more, then add the onion and stir-fry for a further *5 minutes*. Add the curry paste and a little water – enough to loosen the mixture without making it too runny. Add the cashews and ground almonds.

3 Transfer the mixture to a heavy-lidded casserole and stir in the steak and marinade. Cover and bake in a preheated oven, 190°C (375°F), Gas Mark 5, for *20 minutes*.

4 Add the cream and chopped coriander to the casserole and continue cooking for *30 minutes*. If, at the end of cooking there is an excess of oil, spoon it off. Garnish with chopped cashew nuts and coriander.

Preparation time: 15 minutes, plus marinating
Cooking time: about 1 hour
Serves 4

Lamb with Spicy Hot Sauce

Take care. This simple stir-fry is fiery hot.

500 g (1 lb) lamb neck fillet
3 tablespoons groundnut oil
4 spring onions, thinly sliced
    on the diagonal
2 garlic cloves, crushed
bean thread noodles,
    to serve
6–8 small fresh chillies, to
    garnish (optional)

SAUCE:
2 teaspoons cornflour
4 tablespoons cold water
2 tablespoons hot chilli sauce
1 tablespoon rice wine vinegar
    or white wine or cider
    vinegar
2 teaspoons dark soft brown
    sugar
½ teaspoon Chinese five-spice
    powder

1 Wrap the lamb in clingfilm and place it in the freezer for *1–2 hours* until it is just hard. Cut it into thin strips against the grain, discarding any fat and sinew. Leave at room temperature for about *30 minutes* or until the meat has completely thawed.

2 Prepare the sauce. Blend the cornflour to a thin paste with the cold water, then stir in the chilli sauce, vinegar, sugar and five-spice powder.

3 Heat an empty large frying pan or wok until hot. Add 2 table-spoons of the oil and heat until hot. Add the lamb and stir-fry over a high heat for *3–4 minutes* or until browned on all sides. Remove the wok from the heat and tip the lamb and its juices into a bowl.

4 Return the pan to a moderate heat. Add the remaining oil and heat until hot. Add the spring onions and garlic and stir-fry for *30 seconds*. Remove with a slotted spoon.

5 Stir the sauce to mix, pour it into the pan and increase the heat to high. Stir until the sauce thickens, then add the lamb and its juices and the spring onion mixture. Toss for *1–2 minutes* or until piping hot. Serve immediately, with bean thread noodles. Garnish with a few small chillies, if liked.

Preparation time: 10 minutes, plus freezing and thawing
Cooking time: about 10 minutes
Serves 3–4

Noodles, Pasta, Rice and Grains

Delicious pasta, spicy noodles and creamy risottos all including plenty of fresh vegetables and herbs. A satisfying meal, prepared in no time at all. Many of these dishes use a number of basic storecupboard ingredients, combined with fresh fish, seasonal vegetables and herbs and spices, making a delicious, healthy meal in a bowl.

Noodles with Chicken and Prawns

25 g (1 oz) dried shiitake
    mushrooms
175 ml (6 fl oz) hot water
500 g (1 lb) dried egg noodles
2 tablespoons groundnut oil
175 g (6 oz) boneless, skinless
    chicken breast, diced
1 garlic clove, crushed
2 slices fresh root ginger,
    peeled and chopped
4 spring onions, diagonally
    sliced into 1 cm (½ inch)
    pieces

175 g (6 oz) raw prawns,
    peeled
2 tablespoons soy sauce
2 tablespoons rice wine or dry
    sherry
900 ml (1½ pints) Chicken
    Stock (see page 9)
2 tablespoons cornflour
50 g (2 oz) cooked ham,
    shredded
salt

1 Soak the dried shiitake mushrooms in the hot water for *35–40 minutes*. Meanwhile, cook the egg noodles according to packet instructions until they are just tender. Drain and divide between 6 deep bowls. Keep warm.

2 Drain the shiitake mushrooms into a sieve. Slice the mushroom caps thinly.

3 Heat an empty large frying pan or wok until hot. Add the oil and heat until hot. Add the chicken, garlic and ginger and stir-fry over a moderate to high heat for *3–4 minutes*. Add the spring onions and mushrooms and stir-fry for *2 minutes*.

4 Add the prawns, soy sauce, rice wine or sherry, ½ teaspoon salt and the stock. Bring to the boil over a high heat, then simmer for *5 minutes*. Blend the cornflour to a paste with a little cold water, then pour it into the liquid in the pan and stir until it thickens slightly.

5 Pour the chicken and prawns over the noodles, sprinkle with the shredded ham and serve immediately.

Preparation time: 20 minutes, plus soaking
Cooking time: about 20 minutes
Serves 6

Hot and Sour Noodle Salad

A fresh tasting Thai-style salad made with the clear rice noodles available in many larger supermarkets or oriental stores.

½ cucumber, peeled, halved
    and deseeded
50 g (2 oz) vermicelli rice
    noodles
1 carrot, cut into long julienne
    strips
1 red chilli, deseeded and cut
    into long julienne strips
2 tablespoons chopped fresh
    coriander

salt
coriander sprigs, to garnish
DRESSING:
2 tablespoons sunflower oil
½ teaspoon sesame oil
2 teaspoons caster sugar
2 tablespoons lime juice
1 tablespoon Thai fish sauce
    (nam pla)
salt and pepper

1 Sprinkle the cucumber with a little salt and set aside to drain for *30 minutes*. Cover the noodles in boiling water and soak for *4–6 minutes*, or according to the packet instructions. Wash and dry the cucumber and drain and dry the noodles.

2 Combine all the dressing ingredients and season with salt and pepper, to taste. Reserve 2 tablespoons of the dressing and toss the remainder with half the noodles. Place in a large bowl.

3 Cut the cucumber into long thin julienne strips and add to the noodles together with the julienne strips of carrot and chilli. Stir in the coriander and the reserved dressing and serve at once, garnished with coriander sprigs.

Preparation time: 15 minutes, plus draining
Serves 4–6

Crispy Noodles with Mixed Vegetables

50 g (2 oz) dried Chinese
    mushrooms
250 g (8 oz) Chinese cabbage
250 g (8 oz) canned bamboo
    shoots
250 g (8 oz) canned water
    chestnuts

1 onion
1 teaspoon cornflour
2 tablespoons soy sauce
250 g (8 oz) egg noodles
4 tablespoons oil
oil, for deep-frying

1 Soak the Chinese mushrooms in boiling water for *30 minutes*. Drain, reserving the water, and cut into quarters. Shred the cabbage. Thinly slice the bamboo shoots, water chestnuts and the onion. Mix the cornflour with the soy sauce and 4 tablespoons of the reserved mushroom liquid.

2 Cook the noodles in boiling salted water for *15 minutes.* Drain and divide into 4 portions. Heat the oil in a large frying pan or wok, over a high heat. Add the onion and stir-fry for *1 minute*. Add the Chinese cabbage, bamboo shoots, water chestnuts and mushrooms and stir-fry for a further *2 minutes*. Pour in the cornflour mixture and stir until it boils and thickens. Remove the pan from the heat, put the vegetables into a serving dish and keep warm.

3 Heat the oil for deep-frying to 180°C (350°F). Add one portion of the noodles, keeping them together in an even round shape as far as possible. Deep-fry for about *6 minutes* until they are crisp and brown, turning once. Lift out the noodles and drain on kitchen paper. Reheat the oil and cook the remaining noodles in the same way.

4 To serve, put portions of crispy noodles on top of the vegetables.

Preparation time: 15 minutes, plus soaking
Cooking time: about 25 minutes
Serves 4

Creamed Chicken with Tagliatelle

1 tablespoon oil
1 onion chopped
1 garlic clove, crushed
400 g (13 oz) can chopped
    tomatoes
125 ml (4 fl oz) dry white wine
125 ml (4 fl oz) Chicken Stock
    (see page 9)

2 tablespoons chopped basil
375 ml (12 oz) cooked chicken,
    cut into pieces
3 tablespoons crème fraîche
500 (1 lb) fresh tagliatelle
salt and pepper
basil sprigs, to garnish
grated Parmesan, to serve

1 Heat the oil in a saucepan and cook the onion and garlic for *5 minutes*, until softened. Add the tomatoes, wine, stock, basil and salt and pepper. Bring to the boil, then lower the heat. Cover the pan and simmer for *15–20 minutes*. Add the chicken pieces and crème fraîche and heat through.

2 Meanwhile, cook the tagliatelle, according to packet instructions, until tender. Drain thoroughly and transfer to a warmed serving dish. Pour over the sauce and toss thoroughly.

3 Garnish with the basil sprigs and serve with grated Parmesan cheese.

Preparation time: 20 minutes
Cooking time: about 30 minutes
Serves 4

1 Heat about 5 cm (2 inch) of vegetable oil in a heavy-based saucepan to 190°C (375°F), or until a cube of bread browns in *30 seconds*. Add the tofu and fry for *3–4 minutes*, until crisp and lightly golden. Drain the tofu on kitchen paper.

2 Cook the noodles according to the packet instructions, drain, refresh under cold water and dry well on kitchen paper.

3 Blanch the broccoli and sweetcorn in a saucepan of boiling water for *1 minute*, drain, refresh under cold water and pat dry with paper towels. Mix together the soy sauce, lemon juice, sugar and chilli sauce and set aside.

4 Heat the sunflower oil in a large frying pan or wok, add the garlic and chilli and stir-fry for *3 minutes*. Add the noodles and stir-fry for *5 minutes*, until golden and starting to crisp up.

5 Stir in the eggs, and stir-fry for *1 minute*, then stir in the soy sauce mixture, tofu, vegetables and water chestnuts and stir-fry for a further *2–3 minutes* until heated through. Serve at once.

Preparation time: 20 minutes
Cooking time: 15–18 minutes
Serves 4

Egg-fried Noodles with Vegetables and Tofu

vegetable oil, for deep-frying
250 g (8 oz) plain tofu (bean curd), cubed
75 g (3 oz) dried thread egg noodles
125 g (4 oz) broccoli florets
125 g (4 oz) baby sweetcorn, halved
3 tablespoons light soy sauce
1 tablespoon lemon juice
1 teaspoon sugar
1 teaspoon chilli sauce
3 tablespoons sunflower oil
1 garlic clove, chopped
1 red chilli, deseeded and sliced
2 eggs, lightly beaten
125 g (4 oz) drained water chestnuts, sliced

Pasta with Prawns, Peas and Mint Pesto

375 g (12 oz) dried casareccie
   or other pasta shapes
6 tablespoons walnut or olive
   oil
1 leek, sliced
2 garlic cloves, sliced
375 g (12 oz) cooked peeled
   prawns
125 g (4 oz) peas, thawed if
   frozen
4 tablespoons single cream
25 g (1 oz) chopped walnuts,
   toasted

salt and pepper
mint sprigs, to garnish
MINT PESTO:
6 tablespoons chopped mint
1 tablespoon chopped parsley
1 garlic clove, crushed
1 tablespoon freshly grated
   Parmesan cheese
1 tablespoon double cream
1 teaspoon balsamic vinegar
3 tablespoons extra virgin
   olive oil

1 Bring a large saucepan of lightly salted water to the boil, plunge in the pasta, return to the boil and cook for *10 minutes,* or according to the packet instructions, until just tender.

2 Meanwhile, place all the ingredients for the pesto in a food processor or blender and blend until smooth. Season with salt and pepper, to taste.

3 Heat the oil in a large frying pan or wok and stir-fry the leek and garlic for *5 minutes* until softened. Stir in the prawns and peas and heat through.

4 Drain the pasta and stir in the pesto, cream and salt and pepper, to taste, and toss with the prawns and peas. Serve immediately, topped with the walnuts and garnished with mint sprigs.

Preparation time: 5 minutes
Cooking time: 15 minutes
Serves 4

Pappardelle with Pesto and Potatoes

375 g (12 oz) new potatoes or
   large red-skinned potatoes,
   cut into chunks
2 tablespoons olive oil
1 tablespoon coarse salt
300 g (10 oz) fresh pappardelle
250 g (8 oz) ready-made pesto

salt
TO GARNISH:
2 tablespoons toasted pine
   nuts
2 tablespoons finely chopped
   fresh parsley

1 Cook the potatoes in a pan of lightly salted boiling water for *15–20 minutes* until just tender.

2 Drain the potatoes, dry them on kitchen paper, then place them in a shallow dish with the olive oil and salt and toss gently to coat with the oil.

3 Bring at least 1.8 litres (3 pints) water to the boil in a large saucepan. Add a dash of oil and a generous pinch of salt. Add the pasta and cook for *4–8 minutes* or according to packet instructions, until tender.

4 Drain the pasta well and transfer to a warm serving bowl. Add the potatoes and pesto, and toss thoroughly. Garnish with pine nuts and parsley, and serve with a mixed green salad, if liked.

Preparation time: 15 minutes
Cooking time: 20–30 minutes
Serves 4

Vegetable Biryani

250 g (8 oz) basmati rice, rinsed

6 tablespoons sunflower oil

2 large onions, thinly sliced

2 garlic cloves, crushed

2 teaspoons grated fresh root ginger

250 g (8 oz) sweet potato, diced

2 large carrots, diced

1 tablespoon curry paste

2 teaspoons ground turmeric

1 teaspoon ground cinnamon

1 teaspoon chilli powder

300 ml (½ pint) Vegetable Stock (see page 9)

4 ripe tomatoes, skinned, deseeded and diced

175 g (6 oz) cauliflower florets

125 g (4 oz) frozen peas, thawed

50 g (2 oz) cashew nuts, toasted

2 tablespoons chopped fresh coriander

salt and pepper

2 hard-boiled eggs, quartered, to serve

1 Bring a large saucepan of salted water to the boil, add the basmati rice and return to a simmer. Cook gently for *5 minutes*. Drain, refresh under cold water and drain again. Spread the rice out on a large baking sheet and set aside to dry.

2 Heat 2 tablespoons of oil in a frying pan, add half the onion and fry over a medium heat for *10 minutes* until very crisp and golden. Remove and drain on paper towels. Reserve for garnishing.

3 Add the remaining oil to the pan and fry the remaining onion with the garlic and ginger for *5 minutes*. Add the potato, carrots and spices and fry for a further *10 minutes* until light golden.

4 Add the stock and tomatoes, bring to the boil, cover and simmer gently for *20 minutes*. Add the cauliflower and peas and cook for a further *8–10 minutes* until all the vegetables are tender.

5 Stir in the rice, cashew nuts and coriander. Cook, stirring, for *3 minutes*, then cover and remove from the heat. Leave to stand for *5 minutes* before serving with the egg quarters.

Preparation time: 25 minutes
Cooking time: about 1 hour
Serves 4

Pumpkin and Sage Risotto with Pine Nut Sauce

2 tablespoons extra virgin olive oil

1 large onion, finely chopped

1 garlic clove, crushed

1–2 tablespoons fresh sage

400 g (13 oz) arborio rice

375 g (12 oz) pumpkin flesh, diced

1 litre (1¾ pints) simmering Vegetable Stock (see page 9)

50 g (2 oz) pine nuts

50 g (2 oz) freshly shredded Parmesan cheese

4 tablespoons milk

pinch of ground nutmeg

salt and pepper

Parmesan shavings, to serve

sage leaves, to garnish

1 Heat the oil in a large frying pan or wok and fry the onion, garlic and sage for about *5 minutes* until golden. Add the rice and pumpkin and stir-fry for *1 minute* until all the rice grains are well coated in oil.

2 Add a ladleful of stock and simmer, stirring, until absorbed. Gradually add more stock, a ladleful at a time, until the rice is creamy and all the liquid is absorbed, (this will take about *25 minutes)*.

3 Meanwhile, put the pine nuts, cheese, milk and nutmeg in a liquidizer or food processor and blend until smooth. Stir into the risotto, with the final addition of stock, and simmer for a further *5 minutes*. Season to taste and serve at once with Parmesan shavings and garnished with sage leaves.

Preparation time: 20 minutes
Cooking time: 35–40 minutes
Serves 4

1 Scrub the mussels thoroughly under cold running water and discard any that are cracked. Place in a large saucepan with a little water and boil, covered, until they open. Shake the pan occasionally. Strain and set aside, reserving the cooking liquid and discarding any mussels that have not opened.

2 Heat the olive oil in a large deep frying pan. Add the onion and garlic and fry gently until they are soft and golden, stirring from time to time.

3 Stir in the rice and cook over a low heat for *1–2 minutes*, stirring, until the grains are glistening with oil and almost translucent. Pour in some of the fish stock and the reserved mussel liquid and wine and bring to the boil.

4 Meanwhile, soak the saffron in a little boiling water and add to the risotto with the prepared prawns, scallops and squid. Reduce the heat to a simmer and cook gently, adding more fish stock as necessary, until the rice is tender and creamy and all the liquid has been absorbed. Stir in the mussels and season with salt and pepper. Sprinkle with parsley and serve garnished with oregano sprigs.

Preparation time: 25 minutes
Cooking time: 45 minutes
Serves 4–6

Seafood Risotto

500 g (1 lb) fresh mussels in
  their shells
4 tablespoons olive oil
1 onion, chopped
2 garlic cloves, crushed
375 g (12 oz) arborio risotto
  rice
1.8 litres (3 pints) fish stock
125 ml (4 fl oz) dry white wine

few saffron threads
375 g (12 oz) cooked peeled
  prawns
250 g (8 oz) scallops
250 g (8 oz) prepared squid
2 tablespoons chopped
  parsley
salt and pepper
oregano sprigs, to garnish

Risotto alla Parmigiana

125 g (4 oz) unsalted butter,
    softened
1 onion, finely chopped
3–4 tablespoons dry white
    wine
400 g (13 oz) arborio risotto
    rice

1 litre (1¾ pints) simmering
    Beef Stock (see page 9)
125 g (4 oz) freshly grated
    Parmesan cheese
pepper
Parmesan shavings, to
    garnish

1 Melt half the butter in a heavy-based pan, add the onion and fry gently for *5 minutes* until softened. Season with pepper, to taste, then add the wine and boil until it evaporates.

2 Add the rice and cook, stirring, for *1–2 minutes* until it has absorbed the onion and wine mixture. Add a ladleful of the hot stock and cook over a medium heat, stirring, until it has been absorbed. Continue adding the stock, a ladleful at a time, stirring constantly and adding more only when the previous addition has just been absorbed. When all the stock has been absorbed (this will take about *20–25 minutes*), remove the pan from the heat, add the remaining butter and the Parmesan, and fold in gently.

3 Transfer to warmed plates, sprinkle with the Parmesan shavings and a generous grinding of black pepper, and serve immediately with radicchio and rocket leaves.

Preparation time: 5–10 minutes
Cooking time: 35–40 minutes
Serves 4–6

Courgette Risotto

375 g (12 oz) courgettes,
    quartered lengthways and
    cut into chunks
3 tablespoons olive oil
1 small onion, chopped
300 g (10 oz) arborio risotto
    rice

1 litre (1¾ pints) simmering
    Chicken Stock (see page 9)
25 g (1 oz) butter
3 tablespoons freshly grated
    Parmesan cheese
salt and pepper

1 Put the courgettes into a colander and sprinkle with salt. Leave to drain for *30 minutes*, then pat dry on kitchen paper.

2 Heat 2 tablespoons of the oil in a saucepan, add the courgettes and fry until slightly darkened. Remove from the pan and set aside.

3 Heat the remaining oil in the saucepan, add the onion and fry for *5 minutes*, stirring occasionally.

4 Add the rice, stirring, until all the grains are coated with oil. Add a ladleful of the stock and bring to the boil. Simmer until all the liquid has been absorbed. Continue adding the stock in this way until all the liquid has been absorbed and the rice is creamy.

5 Stir in the courgettes, season to taste and heat through. Remove the pan from the heat, and quickly stir in the butter and cheese. Transfer to a warmed serving dish and serve at once.

Preparation time: 5–10 minutes, plus draining
Cooking time: 30–35 minutes
Serves 4

Wild Rice with Cranberries and Pecans

300 g (10 oz) wild rice
2 tablespoons olive oil
1 onion, finely chopped
1 garlic clove, crushed
750 ml (1¼ pints) Chicken
   Stock (see page 9)
2 teaspoons dried mixed herbs

25 g (1 oz) cranberries,
   thawed, if frozen
25 g (1 oz) dried cranberries
25 g (1 oz) pecan nuts, toasted
2 tablespoons chopped fresh
   coriander
salt and pepper

1 Rinse the wild rice thoroughly and then soak in cold water for *1 hour*. Drain.

2 Heat the oil in a large saucepan and fry the onion and garlic until softened but not brown. Add the rice to the pan and coat in the oil. Add the stock and dried herbs, bring to the boil, and simmer, covered, for *40 minutes*.

3 Add the fresh and dried cranberries and pecans and simmer uncovered for a further *5–10 minutes*. If any cooking liquid remains, increase the heat and boil it off. Remove from the heat and stir in the coriander. Season to taste. Serve immediately while still warm. Alternatively, leave to cool completely and serve as a salad.

Preparation time: 20 minutes, plus soaking
Cooking time: 1 hour
Serves 4

Rice with Fontina and Gorgonzola

375 g (12 oz) arborio risotto
   rice
450 ml (¾ pint) milk
15 g (½ oz) butter
40 g (1½ oz) plain flour
150 g (5 oz) Gorgonzola
   cheese, diced

175 ml (6 fl oz) single cream
150 g (5 oz) Fontina cheese,
   rind removed and diced
salt and pepper

1 Boil the rice in plenty of lightly salted water, according to the packet instructions. Drain well.

2 Put the milk in a small pan over a low heat. Soften two-thirds of the butter in a separate pan, add the flour, stirring well, then gradually add the hot milk, stirring continuously to make a sauce. Gradually add the small pieces of Gorgonzola and season with salt and pepper. Remove from the heat and stir in the cream.

3 Place the drained rice in a bowl with the diced Fontina cheese and mix with the remaining butter.

4 Using a third of the rice, make a layer of rice in a buttered oven-proof dish, cover with one third of the Gorgonzola sauce. Repeat the layers with the remaining ingredients, making 2 further layers.

5 Bake the dish in a preheated oven, 180°C (350°F), Gas Mark 4, for *10 minutes*. Serve immediately.

Preparation time: 10 minutes
Cooking time: about 35 minutes
Serves 4

Mexican Rice

250 g (8 oz) long-grain rice
4 tablespoons olive oil
2 garlic cloves, crushed
1 small onion, grated
1 red pepper, cored, deseeded
  and chopped
1 large tomato, skinned,
  deseeded and chopped

1 tablespoon finely chopped
  fresh coriander
1 tablespoon ground cumin
600–750 ml (1–1¼ pints)
  Chicken or Beef Stock (see
  page 9)
salt and pepper
coriander sprigs, to garnish

1 Place the rice in a sieve and rinse thoroughly under cold running water to remove any excess starch. Drain and tip the rice into a large bowl, then cover with hot water. Leave to stand for *30 minutes*.

2 Drain the rice thoroughly in a sieve, and then leave it in the sieve placed over a bowl for about *1 hour* until it is really dry.

3 Heat the oil in a heavy frying pan and add the rice. Cook, stirring, over a low heat until all the grains are well coated with oil, glistening and translucent. Add the garlic and onion and cook until they are transparent and the rice is golden.

4 Add the red pepper, tomato, coriander, cumin and stock. Stir well, cover the pan and cook gently over a very low heat for *20–30 minutes*, until all the liquid has been absorbed and the grains of rice are tender and fluffy. Season with salt and pepper, to taste, and serve hot as an accompaniment to a main dish, garnished with coriander sprigs.

Preparation time: 15 minutes, plus standing
Cooking time: 30–40 minutes
Serves 4

Couscous with Dried Cranberries and Orange Rind

75 g (3 oz) couscous
10 saffron threads, soaked in
  2 tablespoons boiling water
2 tablespoons olive oil
2 large onions, roughly
  chopped
25 g (1 oz) dried cranberries
2 tablespoons toasted,
  blanched almonds
½ tablespoon chopped fresh
  coriander

3 tablespoons grated orange
  rind
1 tablespoon chopped mint
salt and pepper
YOGURT DRESSING:
250 ml (8 fl oz) natural yogurt
2 teaspoons chilli sauce
2 tablespoons olive oil
1 tablespoon lemon juice
1 tablespoon chopped mint

1 Place the couscous in a bowl and add the saffron strands and soaking liquid. Pour over enough boiling water to just cover the couscous. Leave to stand for *10 minutes* to allow the couscous to soak. Toss the couscous with a fork to separate the grains then spoon into a steamer and steam for *10 minutes*, or until done.

2 Heat the oil in a heavy-based saucepan and lightly fry the onions until just golden brown. Add the fried onions, cranberries, almonds and coriander to the couscous and warm through. Remove the couscous from the heat, stir in the orange rind and mint and season to taste with salt and pepper.

3 To make the dressing, mix together all the ingredients in a screw-top jar and serve separately.

Preparation time: 10 minutes, plus standing
Cooking time: 10–12 minutes
Serves 4

Salads and Vegetables

Nothing could be more healthy than a freshly prepared salad. A relaxing summer lunch, a light dinner, or an accompaniment to a meal. The versatile salad and the vegetable side dish are perfect for every occasion.

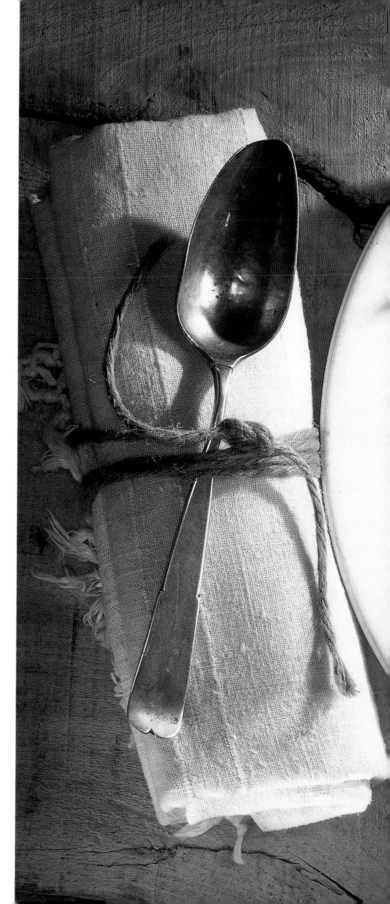

Tuna and Coriander Salad

250 g (8 oz) French beans,
    topped and tailed
425 g (14 oz) can tuna in brine,
    drained
½ red onion, thinly sliced
1 teaspoon finely grated
    lemon rind

handful of coriander leaves,
    roughly torn
1 quantity Classic French
    Dressing (see below)
salt and pepper

1 Bring a saucepan of water to the boil. Add the French beans. Cook for *5 minutes*, then drain. Refresh under cold water, then drain well.

2 Flake the tuna and place it in a large bowl. Add the onion, lemon rind and coriander with salt and pepper, to taste. Pour the dressing over the salad and toss gently.

3 To serve, arrange the tuna salad on a bed of French beans on a serving platter or on individual plates.

Preparation time: 20 minutes
Cooking time: 5 minutes
Serves 4

Classic French Dressing

1 Combine 2 tablespoons of red or white wine vinegar, 1–2 garlic cloves, 2 teaspoons of Dijon mustard and ¼ teaspoon caster sugar in a small bowl. Season with salt and pepper, to taste.

2 Gradually whisk in 6 tablespoons of olive oil. Taste and add more salt and pepper, if necessary.

3 Alternatively, put all the ingredients in a screw-top jar, close the lid tightly and shake well until combined. Use as required.

Makes about 150 ml (¼ pint)
Preparation time: 5 minutes

Salade Niçoise

250 g (8 oz) new potatoes
200 g (7 oz) canned tuna in
    brine, drained and flaked
125 ml (4 fl oz) olive oil
1 tablespoon balsamic vinegar
1 garlic clove, crushed
2 tablespoons capers,
    drained, washed and
    chopped
2 tablespoons chopped basil
1 teaspoon wholegrain
    mustard

4 small eggs
175 g (6 oz) French beans
500 g (1 lb) tomatoes,
    quartered
175 g (6 oz) cucumber, sliced
50 g (2 oz) pitted black olives
50 g (2 oz) anchovies in oil,
    drained
salt and pepper

1 Cook the potatoes in a saucepan of lightly salted, boiling water for *10–12 minutes* until just tender. Drain well, rinse briefly with cold water to stop the cooking process, halve and place in a lowl.

2 Add the tuna to the potatoes. Whisk together the oil, vinegar, garlic, capers, basil, mustard and salt and pepper, to taste. Pour over the tuna and potatoes, cover and marinate for *1 hour*.

3 Meanwhile, bring a saucepan of water to the boil, carefully spoon in the eggs and, timing from when the water returns to the boil, cook the eggs for *6 minutes* for a soft yolk or *8 minutes* for a hard yolk as you prefer. Immediately plunge the eggs into cold water, allow to cool and then shell.

4 Blanch the French beans in a pan of lightly salted, boiling water for *2 minutes*; drain, refresh under cold water and pat dry.

5 Just before serving, put the tomatoes in a large bowl and add the French beans and cucumber. Carefully stir in the potatoes, tuna and all the dressing and transfer to a serving bowl. Quarter the eggs and arrange them over the salad, together with the olives and the anchovies.

Preparation time: 15 minutes, plus marinating
Cooking time: 20–25 minutes
Serves 4

Couscous Salad with Tuna, Raisins and Pine Nuts

250 g (8 oz) couscous
500 g (1 lb) ripe tomatoes, skinned and chopped
125 ml (4 fl oz) extra virgin olive oil
2 tablespoons balsamic vinegar
1 garlic clove, crushed
2 teaspoons ground coriander
½ teaspoon ground cumin
½ teaspoon ground cinnamon
50 g (2 oz) raisins
425 g (14 oz) can tuna in oil, drained and flaked
50 g (2 oz) pine nuts, toasted
2 tablespoons chopped fresh coriander
1 tablespoon chopped mint
salt and pepper

1 Place the couscous in a bowl with the chopped tomatoes. Combine the oil, vinegar, garlic, spices, raisins and salt and pepper to taste and pour over the couscous. Stir well until all the grains are moist, cover and chill in the refrigerator overnight.

2 Remove the bowl of couscous from the refrigerator and leave for *1 hour* to return to room temperature.

3 Stir the tuna into the couscous mixture with the pine nuts and herbs, season with salt and pepper, to taste and serve.

Preparation time: 15 minutes, plus chilling
Serves 4–6

Caesar Salad

2 garlic cloves, crushed
6 tablespoons olive oil
3 slices bread, cut into 5 mm (¼ inch) cubes
2 tablespoons lemon juice
1 teaspoon Worcestershire sauce
1 large cos lettuce, torn into pieces
2 eggs, boiled for 1 minute
4 tablespoons grated Parmesan cheese
salt and pepper

1 Place the garlic in the olive oil and leave to soak for *3–4 hours*. Strain the oil.

2 Fry the croûtons in 4 tablespoons of the garlic-flavoured oil until golden. Drain on kitchen paper.

3 Pour the remaining oil into a small bowl with the lemon juice, Worcestershire sauce, and salt and pepper, to taste and mix well.

4 Put the lettuce into a salad bowl. Pour over the prepared dressing and toss well. Break the eggs over the lettuce, scraping out the partly set egg white, and mix thoroughly to combine the egg with the dressing. Add the cheese and croûtons and give the salad a final toss just before serving.

Preparation time: 10 minutes, plus soaking
Cooking time: 3–4 minutes
Serves 6

Tomato Salad with Anchovies and Cumin

The combined flavours of tomato, mustard, anchovies and cumin make a biting, piquant salad. For a more substantial dish, garnish the salad with slices of hard-boiled egg.

1 heaped teaspoon French
   mustard
2 tablespoons white or red
   wine vinegar
75 ml (3 fl oz) olive oil
4–5 firm tomatoes, sliced
1 red onion, diced

1 celery stick, cut into thin
   finger-length strips
1 teaspoon cumin seeds
2 anchovy fillets, chopped
salt and pepper
2 hard-boiled eggs, to garnish
   (optional)

1 Place the mustard in a small bowl and stir in the vinegar. Season lightly with salt and plenty of pepper. Whisk in the olive oil until the mixture is well blended.

2 Place the tomatoes in a salad bowl with the onion, celery, cumin seeds and anchovy fillets.

3 Pour on the dressing and mix well. Garnish the salad with the hard-boiled eggs, if using, and serve.

Preparation time: 20 minutes
Cooking time: 3–4 minutes
Serves 4

Egg, Croûtons and Cress Salad

oil, for shallow-frying
6 slices white bread, cut into
   1 cm (½ inch) cubes
4 hard-boiled eggs
2 bunches watercress
2 cartons mustard and cress
4 spring onions, chopped
1 green pepper, cored,
   deseeded and chopped

salt and pepper
DRESSING:
50 g (2 oz) blue Brie cheese,
   softened
2 tablespoons mayonnaise
2 tablespoons double cream
1 tablespoon chopped parsley
1 tablespoon snipped chives
pinch of chilli powder

1 Heat the oil in a frying pan, add the croûtons and fry until golden brown. Drain on kitchen paper.

2 Chop the eggs and put them into a large salad bowl. Break the watercress into sprigs and add them to the bowl with the mustard and cress, spring onions and green pepper. Season well with salt and pepper.

3 To make the dressing, put the cheese into a bowl and beat until smooth. Gradually mix in the mayonnaise and cream, then fold in the herbs and chilli powder. Season with salt, to taste.

4 Spoon the dressing over the salad. Add the croûtons, toss well and serve immediately.

Preparation time: 15 minutes
Cooking time: about 5 minutes
Serves 4

Flageolet Bean and Roasted Vegetable Salad

1 aubergine, topped and tailed
1 red pepper, halved, cored
    and deseeded
1 yellow pepper, halved, cored
    and deseeded
1 courgette, topped and tailed
4 garlic cloves, peeled but left
    whole
4 tablespoons olive oil
1 teaspoon coarse sea salt
300 g (10 oz) flagelot beans,
    cooked and drained
2 tablespoons chopped mixed
    herbs (parsley and oregano;
    or coriander and mint)
6 tablespoons Classic French
    Dressing (see page 78)
pepper

1 Cut all the vegetables into strips and place in a roasting tin. Add the garlic. Sprinkle over the oil, sea salt and pepper. Place in a preheated oven, 200°C (400°F), Gas Mark 6, and roast for *40 minutes*. Transfer to a shallow bowl and leave to cool.

2 Add the beans and toss lightly. Stir the herbs into the French dressing, pour over the salad and serve.

Preparation time: 20 minutes, plus cooling
Cooking time: 40 minutes
Serves 4

Stir-fried Mushrooms

Shiitake and button mushrooms are chosen here for the difference in their shapes, textures and flavours, but you can mix and match other types of mushroom according to preference and availability.

2 tablespoons groundnut oil
1 onion, finely chopped
2 carrots, very finely sliced on
    the diagonal
125 g (4 oz) fresh shiitake
    mushrooms, sliced
    lengthways
125 g (4 oz) fresh button
    mushrooms, sliced
    lengthways
4 garlic cloves, finely chopped
4 tablespoons oyster sauce
2 tablespoons rice wine or dry
    sherry (optional)
4 tablespoons cold water
1 bunch chives, coarsely
    chopped
salt and pepper
egg thread noodles, to serve
    (optional)

1 Heat a large frying pan or wok until hot. Add the oil and heat until hot, then add the onion and carrots and stir-fry for *1–2 minutes*. Add the shiitake and button mushrooms, garlic and plenty of salt and pepper and toss vigorously over a medium heat for *2–3 minutes*.

2 Add the oyster sauce and rice wine or dry sherry, if using, then the cold water. Stir-fry for another *3 minutes*, then add half the chives. Toss for *1 minute* only. Serve hot on a bed of egg thread noodles, if liked, sprinkled with the remaining chives.

Preparation time: 10–15 minutes
Cooking time: about 10 minutes
Serves 4–6

1 Soak the chickpeas overnight in cold water.

2 Drain the chickpeas and place in a saucepan with 1 teaspoon of the salt and the whole peeled onion. Cover with cold water, bring to the boil, and boil hard for *10 minutes*. Reduce the heat and simmer, uncovered, for about *45 minutes*, or until the chickpeas are cooked and tender. Drain and reserve the cooking liquid.

3 Put the bacon in a frying pan and fry until the fat starts to run out of the bacon. Add the onions, garlic and red pepper and continue frying until soft. Stir in the remaining salt, the black pepper, chilli, oregano, tomatoes, tomato purée and some of the reserved bean liquid.

4 Add the drained chickpeas and stir well. Simmer for *10 minutes*, stirring occasionally. Serve hot, sprinkled with chopped fresh coriander leaves.

Preparation time: 15 minutes, plus soaking
Cooking time: about 1¼ hours
Serves 4

Spicy Chickpeas

300 g (10 oz) dried chickpeas
1½ teaspoons salt
1 onion, peeled
6 rashers rindless streaky
   bacon, chopped
2 onions, chopped
1 garlic clove, crushed
1 red pepper, cored, deseeded
   and chopped
¼ teaspoon ground black
   pepper

1 small dried hot red chilli,
   crumbled
½ teaspoon dried oregano
300 g (10 oz) skinned and
   chopped tomatoes
2 tablespoons tomato purée
100 ml (3½ fl oz) water or
   reserved bean liquid
2 tablespoons chopped fresh
   coriander

Aloo Chat

500 g (1 lb) potatoes
2 tablespoons vegetable or
   mustard blend oil
1 onion, sliced
1 teaspoon white cumin seeds
1 teaspoon black mustard
   seeds
½ teaspoon fenugreek seeds
2 teaspoons mild curry
   powder or paste

1 tablespoon tomato purée
4 small tomatoes, quartered
1 tablespoon vinegar
1 teaspoon dried mint
1 tablespoon chopped fresh
   coriander
salt

1 Peel the potatoes and dice if they are large. If they are small and new leave them whole with the skins on. Boil them until they are almost cooked, then strain and set aside.

2 Heat the oil in a large frying pan or wok and stir-fry the onion until soft and transparent. Add the cumin, mustard and fenugreek seeds and stir-fry for *1 minute*. Add the curry powder or paste, tomato purée, tomatoes, vinegar and enough water to prevent them from sticking to the pan. Stir-fry for *3–5 minutes* then add the mint, potatoes and coriander. Season with salt, to taste. Serve hot or cold.

Preparation time: 10–12 minutes
Cooking time: about 20 minutes
Serves 4

Gruyère Potatoes

750 g–1 kg (1½–2 lb) evenly
   shaped potatoes, about
   6 cm (2½ inches) long,
   peeled
300 ml (½ pint) double cream
2 teaspoons chopped chives

¼ teaspoon paprika
2 teaspoons finely chopped
   parsley
75 g (3 oz) Gruyère cheese,
   grated
salt and pepper

1 Trim the potatoes so that they are all the same size, then place in a pan and cover with cold water. Add a little salt to taste. Bring to the boil and simmer for *5 minutes*. Drain thoroughly.

2 Butter an 18 cm (7 inch) round casserole or soufflé dish. Arrange the potatoes so that they are standing upright and packed in firmly so they cannot move.

3 Mix together the cream, chives, salt and pepper, paprika and parsley and pour over the potatoes. Sprinkle the cheese over the top so that the potatoes are covered completely. Cook, uncovered, in a preheated oven, 190°C (375°F), Gas Mark 5, for about *1–1¼ hours* or until the potatoes are cooked through and the cheese is crusty and golden brown.

Preparation time: 15 minutes
Cooking time: 1¼–1½ hours
Serves 4

Cook's Tip
This dish needs no last-minute attention and looks and tastes marvellous. If liked, rub a cut clove of garlic around the casserole before it is buttered.

Mixed Bean Sauté with Almonds and Chives

750 g (1½ lb) mixed beans, trimmed and sliced as necessary (broad beans, runner beans, French beans etc.)
2 tablespoons almond or extra virgin olive oil
1 small leek, trimmed, cleaned and sliced
2 garlic cloves, sliced
50 g (2 oz) flaked almonds
2 tablespoons chopped chives
salt and pepper

1 Blanch all the beans together in a large pan of lightly salted, boiling water for *1 minute*. Drain, refresh under cold running water and pat dry on kitchen paper.

2 Heat the oil in a large frying pan or wok, add the leek, garlic and almonds and fry gently for *3 minutes* until softened. Add the beans, stir-fry for *3–4 minutes* until tender and then stir in the chives and salt and pepper. Serve immediately.

Preparation time: 30 minutes
Cooking time: 8–10 minutes
Serves 4

Braised Soya Beans with Shiitake Mushrooms

175 g (6 oz) soya beans, soaked overnight
3 tablespoons extra virgin olive oil
1 garlic clove, chopped
1 teaspoon grated fresh root ginger
2 red chillies, deseeded and chopped
125 g (4 oz) shiitake mushrooms, sliced
4 ripe tomatoes, skinned, deseeded and chopped
2 tablespoons dark soy sauce
2 tablespoons dry sherry
250 g (8 oz) spinach leaves, washed and shredded

1 Drain the beans and place in a saucepan with plenty of cold water. Bring to the boil and boil rapidly for *10 minutes*, then lower the heat, cover and simmer for *1 hour* or until the beans are tender. Drain, reserving 150 ml (¼ pint) of the cooking liquid.

2 Heat the oil in a large frying pan, add the garlic, ginger and chillies and fry for *3 minutes*. Add the mushrooms and fry for a further *5 minutes* until tender.

3 Add the tomatoes, beans, the reserved liquid, soy sauce and sherry and bring to the boil. Cover and simmer for *15 minutes*.

4 Stir in the spinach and heat through for *2–3 minutes* until the spinach is wilted. Serve immediately.

Preparation time: 15 minutes
Cooking time: about 1½ hours
Serves 4–6

1 Heat 2 tablespoons of the oil in a saucepan, add the onion, garlic, ginger and ground spices, and fry over a medium heat for about *5–6 minutes* until the onion is lightly browned.

2 Place the pumpkin in a bowl, add the curry paste and toss well to coat the pumpkin evenly.

3 Add the tomatoes, chillies and stock to the onion mixture, bring to the boil and simmer gently for *15 minutes*.

4 Meanwhile, heat the remaining oil in a non-stick frying pan, add the coated pumpkin and fry for *5 minutes* until golden. Add to the onion and tomato sauce with the chickpeas, cover and cook for *20 minutes* until the pumpkin is tender.

5 Peel the banana, slice thickly and stir into the curry *5 minutes* before the end of the cooking time. Stir in the chopped coriander and serve immediately with rice and naan bread, if liked.

Preparation time: 10–15 minutes
Cooking time: about 45 minutes
Serves 4

Pumpkin, Chickpea and Banana Curry

Although this combination of flavours might sound unusual, it produces a really tasty dish to serve with plain or spiced rice.

3 tablespoons sunflower oil
1 small onion, sliced
2 garlic cloves, chopped
2 teaspoons grated fresh root ginger
1 teaspoon ground coriander
½ teaspoon ground cumin
½ teaspoon ground turmeric
¼ teaspoon ground cinnamon
625 g (1¼ lb) pumpkin, peeled, deseeded and cut into cubes
2 tablespoons hot curry paste

2 ripe tomatoes, chopped
2 dried red chillies
300 ml (½ pint) Vegetable Stock (see page 9)
375 g (12 oz) canned chickpeas, drained
1 large under-ripe banana
1 tablespoon chopped fresh coriander
TO SERVE:
plain boiled rice
naan bread (optional)

Black Bean Chilli

250 g (8 oz) dried black kidney
beans, soaked overnight
1.5 litres (2½ pints) water
4 tablespoons extra virgin
olive oil
250 g (8 oz) small mushrooms,
halved
1 large onion, chopped
2 garlic cloves, crushed
2 large potatoes, cubed
1 red or green pepper, cored,
deseeded and diced
2 teaspoons ground coriander
1 teaspoon ground cumin
2 teaspoons chilli powder

450 ml (¾ pint) passata (sieved
tomatoes)
1 tablespoon lime juice
25 g (1 oz) chocolate, chopped
2 tablespoons chopped fresh
coriander
AVOCADO SALSA:
1 small ripe avocado
4 spring onions, finely
chopped
1 tablespoon lemon juice
1 tablespoon chopped fresh
coriander
salt and pepper

1 Drain the beans, place in a pan with the water and bring to the boil. Boil rapidly for *10 minutes* then reduce the heat, cover and simmer for *45 minutes*.

2 Meanwhile, heat 2 tablespoons of the oil in a large saucepan and stir-fry the mushrooms for *5 minutes*. Remove from the pan and reserve. Add the remaining oil to the pan with the onion, garlic, potatoes, pepper and spices and fry over a medium heat for *10 minutes*.

3 Drain the beans, reserving the liquid. Boil the liquid until reduced to 450 ml (¾ pint). Stir the beans into the pan with the vegetables, add the stock, passata and mushrooms. Bring to the boil, cover and simmer for *30 minutes*.

4 Meanwhile, make the avocado salsa. Peel, stone and finely dice the avocado and combine with the remaining ingredients. Season with salt and pepper, to taste, cover and set aside.

5 Stir the lime juice, chocolate and coriander in to the pan and cook for a further *5 minutes*. Serve piping hot.

Preparation time: 20 minutes, plus soaking
Cooking time: about 1½ hours
Serves 4 as a starter

Baby Vegetable Stir-fry with Orange and Oyster Sauce

2 tablespoons olive or
walnut oil
175 g (6 oz) baby carrots
175 g (6 oz) whole baby
sweetcorn cobs
175 g (6 oz) small button
mushrooms
salt and pepper

SAUCE:
2 tablespoons cornflour
4 tablespoons water
finely grated rind and juice of
1 large orange
2 tablespoons oyster sauce
1 tablespoon dry sherry or
sherry vinegar

1 To make the sauce, blend the cornflour in a jug with the water, then add the orange rind and juice, oyster sauce and sherry or vinegar. Stir well to combine.

2 Heat a large frying pan or wok until hot. Add the oil and heat over a moderate heat until hot but not smoking. Add the carrots and sweetcorn and stir-fry for *5 minutes*, then add the mushrooms and stir-fry for *3–4 minutes*.

3 Pour in the sauce mixture and bring to the boil over a high heat, stirring constantly until thickened and glossy. Add salt and pepper to taste, garnish with parsley and serve immediately.

Preparation time: 12 minutes
Cooking time: 12–15 minutes
Serves 4–6

Photo Credits:
Octopus Publishing Group Ltd., Bryce Attwell, Steve Baxter, Simon Butcher, Nick Carman, Jean Cazals, Chris Crofton, Laurie Evans, Gus Filgate, Robert Gordon, Christopher Hill, Graham Kirk, Sandra Lane, William Adams-Lingwood, David Loftus, Diana Miller, Paul Moon, Hilary Moore, Vernon Morgan, James Murphy, Peter Myers, Sean Myers, Simon Smith, Charlie Stebbings, Clive Streeter, Ian Wallace, Philip Webb, Paul Williams

Jacket Photography:
David Loftus (front), Ian Wallace (back)
Back Jacket Home Economist:
Sunil Vijayakar